COMMUNICATION IS A FAMILY GAME

How To Reduce Stress and Fighting To Create Harmony at Home

Rebecca Harper

10-10-10
Publishing

COMMUNICATION IS A FAMILY GAME
HOW TO REDUCE STRESS AND FIGHTING TO CREATE HARMONY AT HOME
www.familycomgame.com

Publisher
10-10-10 Publishing
Markham, ON   Canada

Printed in Canada and the United States of America

Table of Contents

Dedicated to my daddy,
Mr. William Finlason,
son, brother, husband, father, uncle, friend, inspiration
(1945 – 2012)

Dear Daddy,
I dedicate this book to you, because I am the mother and philanthropist I am today because of you. You taught me to respect and love everything on this earth, and to always find the good in people and nature. Daddy, as I wrote this book, I could hear your words and feel your inspiration. You taught me to be balanced and to love my three children the same even though I like them differently. I miss you.

"Imagine," by John Lennon

Imagine all the people
Living life in peace
You may say that I'm a dreamer
But I'm not the only one
I hope someday you'll join us
And the world will be as one

Rebecca Harper

Acknowledgements

First and foremost, I would like to thank my three children, **Christopher, Mckenzie,** and **Benjamin**. You have been my inspiration for this book and have been my teachers. You have not only helped me to become a better parent but also a better woman. Thank you.

Next, I'd like to thank my family, my village, my brother and sister-in-law and their family. **Andrew Finlason**, you're an amazing man and an amazing father, husband, and brother. I am blessed to have you in my life, and I thank you for everything you've done for me. **Ali Finlason**, thank you for making my brother a better man, and for introducing me to your mother, **Mrs. Esta Medina,** who I try to emulate, Mrs. Medina, you sat with me as I went through the hardest time of my life, you smiled and told me how much you admired me. You taught me how highlighting my strengths, instead of highlighting their mistakes, can help someone through their hardest times more than negativity. Thank you.

My sister, **Lynda Edwards,** and her husband, **Tim, who** are my village. Thank you for being caring adults to my three children. You took my son when I needed him to have a place to be loved, even though he was spoilt.

My mother and father, **Gladys and William Finlason**, I wouldn't have learned what to do as a parent, and what not to do as a parent, without you. You helped me, formed me, and raised me, but most of all, you loved me. Thank you.

To my best friend, who is more like a sister to me, **Maria Azar**, her three children, **Brandon, Alexandra, and Adam,** and her husband, **Andrew**; you and your family have been there for my family and me, every day of my life, from the moment we were breastfeeding our boys together. Thank you for being in my village, and for supporting my village in every way. You're an amazing mother who has raised amazing children, who support my children, especially Alexandra, who has grown beyond her years and has always been there for my daughter, Mckenzie. Thank you.

Thank you to those people who helped me when the rules of my game changed so drastically. To my friends who helped my children and me at that time, who motivated me and believed in me when I didn't believe in myself. **PB Scott** and **Jen Scott, and Melanie Subrati,** thank you for always motivating me and inspiring me, giving me a chance to start over. **Christopher Dunkley,** mistaken identity goes a long way. Thank you for helping me be a good mother during a hard divorce. When I moved to Canada, it was a hard thing for me to do, and I want to thank all my family, **Aunt Joan, Mark, Ian** and **Brian Davidson;** and to the Finlason Clan, **Wendy, Timmy, Mathew** and **Uncle Howard**, thank you for picking up the mantel—missing Daddy isn't as hard because of you. Thank you all for making that move so easy for me; I couldn't have done it without you.

Next, to all of those bosses who mentored me, believed in me, and knew I could do it at a time when I didn't think I could. Thank you to **Kenny Benjamin, Sheila Benjamin,** and **Valerie Juggan-Brown**. You gave me the freedom to make mistakes and succeed. You were all more mentors to me than bosses. Thank you so much; I learnt many, many things from each of you, and I truly appreciated the two years of growth and guidance that you gave me. Sheila, you taught me how to look at things with a beautiful and artistic eye. Your gentle, loving spirit was so embracing when I needed it the most; thank you for your friendship and your guidance. Mister B, I could not have asked to be mentored by a better man. You believed in me, and you knew when to hold me back or push me forward with a very gentle approach, which is what I needed. I was blessed to have you in my life at that time, so thank you. Valerie, you became a second mother to me; you taught me so much and inspired me every day to be great. You're a big reason why I believed in myself to write this book. Thank you.

My Hope Zoo Preservation Foundation team, what a great team that I had the privilege of leading. In retrospect, I learned so much from each and every one of you; because you trusted me, and the changes we made together. However, the biggest pride I felt was from watching all of you take the initiative to make it better than I imagined. Ideas are no good unless actioned, and it takes a team to make them great. **Chevelle James, Sarah Rieback, Rochelle DeSousa, Neico Knight, and Milton Rieback,** thank you for bringing the zoo to the future, and for teaching the zookeepers the modern way of a zoo. Our vision came to fruition, and it is so nice to see. **Damian Morris (Pants), Andre Myrie, Jodian Blissett, Saddam Quarrie, Shanique Lewis (Antz), Okema Pinnock, Chase Williams , Ryan Baugh (Bottle), Michael Benjamin (Benji), Imani Jones, Vanesha Hinds, Shaneka Howell, Suzette Hughes (Suzie), Sophia Donaldson, Denise James, Gilbert McIntosh (Mackie), Shawn Thompson (Shango), Michael Thompson, Hugh Walker (Capo), Alphonso Francis, Collin Anglin, Sebert Gordon, Hilton Davis, Cherene Rowe, Roden (Security).** My Serengeti team!!!! **Tyrone Simpson, Michael, Carissa Wint, Romar Peart, Keswick Johnson, Almassy Hailey, Tavin Horton (TVJ), Gawain Reid (Puss), Rowan Wedderburn, Herline O'Conner, Tamara Campbell, Alvin Brown, Orlando Robinson, Dr. Andrew Trawford (Doc), and Jeanette Williams.**

My teachers at Seneca, who actually gave me the confidence to write this book: **Phil Edwards,** my mentor in Interpersonal Communication, and my coaching partner and co-host, thank you for believing in the crazy ideas that your past student asked you to do, and for making it happen! **Louisa Iannaci,** your course identified how to communicate in a group, and helped me to explain how my family group works and does not work. I learnt so much about myself in your class. **Azadeh Razbani-Tehrani, thank you** for teaching me about all different types of families, and always encouraging me with my ideas. To have someone as smart and experienced as you tell me how good I am, and respect my experience, gave me the confidence to write. **Benoit Tardiff**, thank you for making me better and for pushing me to ask questions. Thank you! I also want to really thank my Wolfpack at Seneca: **Miriam Karimi, Jackie Mercado**, and **Malalay Sahibzada**. Thank you for having my back in school, and thank you for being such good friends to me, but most of all, thank you for helping and supporting me during my presentations and projects so that I could work on my book. Also, thank you for helping me study for exams once I finished the book and had to pass my exams. Thank you so much for being my friends and my new pack; you have made moving to Canada easier.

Thank you to **Minister Floyd Green** for nominating me for the two boards that I was honoured to serve on, from which I learnt so much. Thank you to my fellow board members on the ECC board: **Mrs. Trisha Williams-Singh, Mrs. Karlene DeGrasse-Deslandes, Mrs. Rosalee Gage-Grey, Mrs. Brittany Singh-Williams, Mrs. Nicole McLaren; Ms. Rachael McDonald, Mrs. Barbara Gooden, Mr. Denzil Thorpe, Mrs. Marcia Reid-Grant, Mr. Easton Williams, and Dr. Elizabeth Ward.** Thank you to my fellow board members on the Child Protection and Family Services Agency board: **Georgia Hamilton, Violet Foster Russell, Lynda Mair, Karl Whyte, and Orville Black**. I cannot leave out the amazing team of the CPFSA, **Mrs. Waller, Mr. Williams, and Ms. Budai.** Keep healing and improving our nation; I look forward to working with you again.

I have to thank the people that recognized my vision and gave me the chance to coach parents on a national level. The team at Nationwide News Network: **Liz Bennet, Mr. Cliff Hughes** and **Lennie Gordon.** Thank you for giving me that spot which ended up at this point of writing a book. Then I cannot leave out RJR Communications

Group team who took my show to the next level and more. **Francois St. Juste** (who was also a mentor), **Derrick Wilkes,** a great mentor and friend, **Kalisha Lawrence,** who saw all my talents and put them to good use! **Dennis Howard, Gary Allen, Judith Alberga** who all encouraged me and motivated me in this field. To the production team and engineers, **Peter Brown, Jeffrey Brown, Tony Hollness, Charles Lannaman** and **Richard Nembhard,** you always made me and my work sound good!

Raymond Harlall, Michael McBean, and the amazing **Dr. Clyde Rivers**, thank you for discovering me, and thank you for where you are taking me. You are helping me to fulfill my purpose in this world, and this book was just the start. I am so excited to be part of the IChange Nations movement.

More importantly, I thank **Mr. Raymond Aaron**, *New York Times* top 10 bestselling author. Thank you for writing the foreword for my book, and helping me to believe in my talent and knowledge on parenting, as well as for the amazing 10-10-10 program you've developed. I thought I could never write a book, but look at me now; I have written a book, thanks to your program. Thank you to your team, **Lisa Browning** (editor) **Naval Kumar** (book architect), **Waqas Ahmed** (genius book cover artist), as well as **Lisa Playfair** (my friend for reading and editing) for assisting me with my book. **Liz, Christina** and **Aysha,** thank you for your advice, and thank you for motivating me, and for all the support you gave me while I was writing my book. Thank you.

There are many more people I could thank, but time, space, and modesty compel me to stop here.

About REBECCA

Rebecca is a communications professional, with almost twenty years experience in the development of strategic national communications plans, spanning various industries.

Born in Mandeville, Jamaica, Rebecca is a mother of three children, and a graduate of Concordia University in Montreal, Canada, with a specialization in communication studies. She recently completed her diploma in social work at Seneca College, and was a justice of the peace in Jamaica. Rebecca simply loves her family and her country.

Her passion in community development, education, and nation building has led her to promote children's rights, rehabilitation of youth, and community development. She produces, writes, and hosts the number one parenting show in Jamaica, *Parent to Parent*, and is also the writer and producer of *RG Kids,* a children's show, on RJR 94 FM.

In addition, the Hope Zoo Preservation Foundation allowed her to extend her passion for animals and the environment, and she developed national educational, family, and environmental projects. Prior to moving to Canada to give her children the opportunities to succeed, she sat on various boards in Jamaica, including The Child Protection and Family Services Agency, Early Childhood Commission, and Natural History Museum.

Currently, Rebecca has her own online courses and parenting YouTube channel, www.interpersonalparenting.com, where she helps and advises parents, and travels to developing countries, establishing family commissions and programs to build strong families and strong nations. She has recently been appointed Ambassador of World Civility. Her Family Civility Initiative promotes every country to celebrate National Family Civility Day which recognizes family diversity with civility.

Rebecca lives by Maya Angelou's quote: *"I've learned that people will forget what you said, people will forget what you did, but people will never forget how you made them feel."*

Foreword

Do you go to bed every night wondering why your children cause you so much stress, or why you were fighting about cleaning a dish? Have you ever wondered how you can get your children through a tough time while you are trying to cope with a tough time yourself? Have you felt that what you say is taken the wrong way and they just don't understand you? If you are like most parents, you probably have. And you are not alone. Perhaps you spend more time screaming at your kids when you get home after a long tiring day than you do relaxing. How can you enjoy your limited time with your kids, instead of worrying and arguing with them?

Rebecca Harper has overcome a life-changing event and found a way to reduce stress and fighting in her home, even with children with exceptionalities and as a single mother. When she speaks you can sense that she has figured it out! Rebecca's vision is a world where every member of the family is doing their thing, living their life purpose, being happy doing it, feeling extraordinary and finding their role in their family.

In this book, you will find very simple ideas, guidelines and suggestions that you can follow to empower you to transform your family and help everyone to communicate in a positive way. Start applying this now and move towards a peaceful life, and bring your family closer together while having fun together. I'm sure there are many ideas and suggestions in this book that will resonate with you.

Raymond Aaron
New York Times Bestselling Author

Chapter 1

HOW I LEARNT TO PLAY THE GAME

I played the family games from the day I was born till now, where I play my own family games. We even teach our babies to play the game and to communicate from day one. Crying means four things for a baby: hunger, discomfort (dirty diaper), need for attention/love, or being sick. We teach them from the beginning there is a response for everything we say and do, that when they cry, we respond. By my third child, I could predict most of the needs, and he of course cried less, and he did not need to tell me when something was wrong. As we grow older, we learn to speak, and even though our desires are the same, the things that fulfill these desires grow and change. We, as people, have the need to be loved, to be comfortable, to eat, and to be healthy, but how we communicate these needs changes as we grow and learn.

Your family is your primary group, it is the first group that teaches you about life and how to interact with other people, especially how to communicate. Most importantly, it is the group that you feel you belong to, which every human being wants to feel. If you don't feel that sense of belonging in that primary group, you tend to feel lost in life, and many emotional issues happen after that. Being the third child, and so young, it was very difficult for me to feel a sense of belonging in my family. Understanding these personalities and family dynamics later in life has allowed me to learn how to communicate better with my family, reducing the hostility and increasing the harmony.

I grew up in a family of different religions, and as a minority, and I always said that I was never on the right side. I am a Christian Jew and a white Jamaican. I grew up in a country where our motto is, *"Out of many, one people."* My father always taught me to love, and to be compassionate and understanding of everyone I meet, no matter their background, and to treat everyone with the same respect and love. I grew up in a country where poor people were in abundance—there is a small middle class—and I saw poverty in its true sense. Even though I was different in so many ways from the rich and the poor, and the Christians and the Jews, I was always accepted—but I was always aware of how different I was.

Being on the wrong side of culture made me more of an observer than a participant, and this allowed me to see how our cultures shape how we think, and how they form us into the people we become, from a very early age. Our parents told us stories of how we were treated in Jamaica due to our class and colour. When I was 10 months old, we were forced to move from Jamaica and migrate to Canada. I then moved back to Jamaica with my family, at 6 years old, from the culture of my upbringing to the culture of my birth. I went against the upper-class mentality of my mother, and embraced the all-class mentality of my father. This created inner conflict on many occasions. I'll go into this later on in the book, when I talk about my authentic self with my friends and people I knew who would accept me, versus my self-image that I had to portray, especially with my mother. This would influence how I communicated and played my personal strategy in my family game. I see so many parents benefit from the self-concept game in my online course, Interpersonal Parenting; I see them finding themselves at the same time as finding out who their children are. I love to see the immediate change in the next week, or their feedback on how the family communicates, creating harmony at home. (Hint: The game is a free bonus.)

I was born seven years later than my siblings, in a family that was already a nuclear family: mother, father, daughter, and son. I was always too young to play the game, so I got the chance to observe more than participate. However, I later found out that this was a blessing and not a curse, as it allowed me to observe how a family communicates. I saw the good, the bad, and the ugly. I also learned how family dynamics, different personalities of the players, and their personal strategies and personal goals can affect the outcome of each family game, which can end with harmony or hostility.

An example of this was when my mother would always try to solve the problems my brother and sister would argue about. By getting involved, she was creating a triangle of communication that was more about getting the third person on their side. Then she would add in the favoritism of my brother, so my poor sister never won the arguments. This eventually led to hostility, and my brother and sister never actually discussed the problem. This encouraged my siblings and me to disconnect later in life. We were taught a way of communication that was not healthy, and it ended up in miscommunication because, even when my mother was not involved, we created the triangle amongst ourselves. For example, my sister and I would have a disagreement, and we would include my brother in order to get his alliance, not to solve the problem, causing more hostility than harmony. I also learnt to never go to the person I had conflict with but to go to a third party, which always ended badly for me, even in my workplace environment.

As a result of this, When I became a parent, my approach was not to get involved. I promise you, I did not learn that right away. We tend to become our mothers and our fathers in our parenting, without knowing it. Self-awareness as a parent is extremely important when it comes to this family game. Many times, we need to break the cycles of parenting through knowledge and reading; and so many times, as I teach them, I learn just as much from the parents I coach and the workshops I do. Communication is always a two-way street; there is a speaker and a listener. Once you learn to do both—to speak and to listen (not at the same time nor in that order)—your life becomes so much easier as a parent. This is something I will help you with in this book. By teaching my children to communicate amongst each other, I also learned how to communicate with them. The other effect was that I also taught them, and myself, how to communicate with the outside world.

The conflict of siblings is another game that I call the *triangle game of communication*. The role of mediator and negotiator helps the triangle, against the role of taking sides and wanting to be the problem solver. My father, being a farmer, would always relate every family issue and experience to something to do with farming. For example, when he and my brother were clashing as my brother became a teenager, he would always step back and say that they were two bulls in a pen, and you can never have two bulls in a pen. My brother would speak to me about the argument, and so would my father. I was caught in the middle, and always found myself mediating or translating.

I took a different role than my mother, and actually translated. In a way, it was like the game, Chinese Telephone, which I was very good at. I would create harmony instead of hostility, because instead of feeling that I was an authority to solve the problem, I encouraged the two people to solve the problem. As an adult, I also thought that this would work out in my role as a parent. However, it completely changed (Sorry Mom, I can understand now.). As a child, communicating between two people is a completely different role than that of a parent, because your children, though you're explaining both sides of the story, actually think you are taking sides. Where I thought I was a mediator and would go to my son, Benjamin, to explain why Mckenzie, my daughter, would act the way she did, I did it in separate rooms like I learnt from my family, instead of together; so each thought that I was taking sides with the other in these private conversations (so that is why my siblings and I had issues!!!). I am fortunate to have a son who is very verbal and will call me out on my stuff; and when he did, because I am an active listener to my kids, and not just a speaker, I realized that he was right, so I changed my tactic.

I played the triangle game, but now I had everyone in the same room, like a normal mediator. This worked very well because my son was now able to hear his version being told to my daughter, and my daughter was able to hear her version being told to him, and they no longer thought I was taking sides. So, it's not just how you play the game, it is where you play the game as well.

There is a great practical way to learn how to play the positive triangle game, and I have created a game that the family can play, in my online parenting course. I actually put games of scenarios, and create the three-player triangle game. I find it works very well to teach parents to not be the problem solver but the mediator, and by using mediation and negotiation tools, you help each person to understand the other, before using it as a teaching moment. Going back to the basics of communication, there is the sender and the receiver. Let me explain: You are with someone, and you are enjoying your surroundings. You mention how the skies are blue, the sun is shining, the birds are singing, and what a beautiful day it is. However, the person who is listening might not be hearing that meaning or the appreciation of the day you are having, because it's not only what you say; it's also HOW you say it. If I say the same sentence in a miserable voice, the receiver could think that I'm being sarcastic because, yes, the sun is shining, but it could be really hot and humid outside; and yes, the birds are singing, but it could be an annoying sound that a blackbird makes, and even though I say that it is a beautiful day, I could sound sarcastic just because of HOW I say it. On the flip side, I could say it with a great tone and a happy voice; however, the receiver could be thinking something different, as they are the one who is hearing the blackbird as an annoying sound. They are the one that actually hates the sun, and they prefer the rain or winter. They're too hot, and therefore they think you're being condescending to them because that's how they feel about the day. Or, when a listener turns to you and maybe shouts at you; you're confused and, in return, get mad at them: "What did I say to have you give a bad response?" That, my friend, is the core of communication—a game we constantly play.

When we play any game, we're always trying to predict what the other is doing so that we can do something else to beat them. But how about we change our strategy by figuring out how the other person thinks, or appreciate that we can never understand how the other person thinks, and communicate as if we respect their personal view? A lot of times, we communicate based on our view and desire to be right, as opposed to communicating for compromise or compatibility. Everyone has a different perspective, based on their past experiences and their personal outlook on life.

I always say, in my parent workshops, "My children all come out of the same place, but they're completely different people." How I deal with one does not work with the others the same way. The first thing I did as a parent to improve communication at home, was to turn the arguments from fighting to harmony, was to learn who my children were as individuals—who they are, not who I wanted them to be. So now I'm going to introduce my three muses for this book. Christopher is my eldest child. He is my athlete, my listener, my observer, and my analyser. In Chapter 3, I'll get more into how he influenced me to be a better person. My daughter, McKenzie, is artistic, creative, an amazing baker, and is my easiest child, even though we had a rough start, as she has Autism. In fact, she has been my teacher; I have not been hers. I can say that I am blessed to have her in my life, as she not only helped me to be a better parent, but she also helped me to be a better person. My youngest is Benjamin, my checks and balances, my little sociologist. He's still in formation stage, and I'm still learning how to play the game, especially as a third and youngest child; however, he got in the game much faster than the other two. I have had to learn who they are, as my descriptions above do not define them; they just help me to strategize how I communicate with them.

I even had to change my strategies with every game of communication. Have you ever played the game, Monopoly? Sometimes we want Boardwalk and the Greens, to win the game, but what happens when another player has the same strategy and beats you to it? You have to change strategies. I'm learning how to win the communication game with completely different strategies. Since my children do come from me, with a bit of their father, sometimes they're going to have the same strategy I do. Just like in a game, you have to figure out the other person's strategy by actively listening. Actively listening means not just hearing what the person says but also observing their body language, eye contact, and everything they're saying. Remember my story about the beautiful day? If we had actively listened to the other person's tone and had observed the smile on their face and their excitement as they looked around, we would have observed that they were listening in a good way. But if you were not *actively* listening to the person, and they had their own perception and their own strategy that they were actually already miserable while they were listening to you, you would be surprised when they argued back. So, as a speaker, you actually have to actively listen before you speak, and observe the person you're speaking to—their mood, their body language, eye contact—before you say what you need to say. Otherwise, we're so quick to speak that we lose the game.

For example, when anything breaks in my house (my kids don't intentionally break things, and it's more than likely an accident), I have a rule: If they hide it from me and lie about it, that's when they're in trouble; but if they come and openly communicate with me about what happened, and why it happened, and they accept responsibility for it, then I actually don't punish them, because they've already learned what not to do.

So many times, we tell our kids not to run in the house and not to play ball in the house, but depending on their age, they haven't had that experience of something breaking. So, their perspective is, "Why does Mommy tell me to do this when nothing has ever happened when I do it?" You may tell them not to play ball in the house and not to run in the house because something will break again, but it has never happened to them, so why should they believe you? However, if I say, "Listen, I remember when I was your age and I played ball in the house, and when I broke my mother's crystal glasses, I got in so much trouble. If you play ball in the house and you break something, you're going to be in trouble because you didn't listen to me." Then you can proceed from there if they've disobeyed you, and say, "Hey, I broke it; I heard you. I know you told me that story, but Mom, I won't play ball in the house again because, yes, it has happened to me as well." I use that as a teaching moment (thank you, Kevin Leman). I say, "Now, do you understand what I am saying?"

So many times, we speak to our children, and they actually don't believe us because, again, it hasn't happened to them. They'll even think that just because it happened to Mommy or it happened to Daddy, it doesn't mean that it will happen to them. Are you going to create an argument, fighting and showing them up, and letting them respond back like that, closing that mode of communication? Or do you create harmony by sitting down and saying, "See, I told you it was going to happen, because—guess what—it happened to me, and it can happen to you. By not having that argument about that harmony that we have created, and opening up the lines of communication (because, again, they came to me about it, and they didn't lie because I always catch it), then they are prone to come to me for everything. Later on in life, you learn that they come to you with everything, even things you don't want them to come to you with (many TMI moments with my oldest son).

However, I want to communicate with my children, and you have heard me say it before that having a child with autism has made me a better parent. Having three children with dyslexia means that they think differently. Scrabble is a game that I love to play, but in Canada, I have no one to play with, and it helps me to think differently on how to communicate with my children. Because of my daughter, I had access to many psychologists, psychiatrists, and neurologists, and mini consultations with teachers. My village partners were a large group that included both positive and negative people. I was told that I was a bad mother, that I don't punish my children enough, and that my parenting styles were lacking because nobody in my family or my husband's family knew about autism, and neither did I. However, having to teach your daughter to communicate on a constant basis taught me mistakes that I was making, not only with her but also with my two boys. I lived in a country where knowledge was expensive or non-existent about autism and dyslexia, and I appreciated the advantages I had.

So, after the hard work, of which I will talk a lot about in this book, I started a radio show, which lasted eight years, helping parents and listening to parents on how to improve their child's behavior. After years of parent coaching, doing my radio show, and implementing national projects for children and parents, I learnt that telling someone how to parent their child my way is just tips, because my children are completely different from each other—they came from the same place, but they have their own issues. What might work for one child doesn't work for the other, so how can it work for other people's children who have different perspectives and life experiences? What I did learn is that the common tool that all parents have is communication—interpersonal communication—which is the basic tool we need in order to stop the fighting and arguing, and to create harmony at home. Choose more depth, and use the actual tools that my listeners and I used in my online course, Interpersonal Parenting.

Chapter 2

HOW I TEACH THE GAME

I always say that the biggest mistake (not really a mistake) I have made in life was to give birth to children that are smarter than I am. But the true mistake that I make at times is by not staying smarter than they are, and by being lazy and relying on my power and authority as a parent, instead of being a better person and teaching them. Hey, we are all tired and have a million things to do. Women have the second shift; we have a full-time career and then come home to work again. We are always being scrutinized by wanting to have it all, and we are always balancing being a "good mother" and being a "good woman." We are always judged on how we play our game, by other women.

Back to my smart children, even though we all play the same game, I have had to teach it differently to each child, and they get smarter each year—sometimes each month—and I have to constantly teach it a different way at different times. I teach them, like anything else, when you play a game or when you are playing a game with others who have not played the game before, you usually read the rules first, try a sample game, or play a game to show them how it's done, and then you play a real game. My family isn't any different. I teach the game of the supermarket, for example, and yes, every life experience is a game, and many people think of it as a derogatory term. Life's a game, and life is fun, so why can't we play games every day? Children play games to learn social cues on the playground. They learn to take turns. Playing Marco Polo teaches our children how to listen and how to not make noise so that Marco can't find them, and how to move quickly in order to respect the rule that when Marco calls his name, you have to reply, "Polo."

Everything I did with my children, I made it into a game. My favorite game, especially with my children, was a game I played when my daughter was 3 years old. I was just learning how to handle a child with autism, at a time when parents and doctors knew very little about it. What I know now, I could really have used 10 years ago. I am sure that everyone can relate to temper tantrums in the supermarket, and if you have escaped this game, then please tell me your secret. If you escaped it with all your children, then kudos to you. My daughter helped me realize that it was my lack of planning, my lack of routine (which I called spontaneity), and especially my lack of knowledge on how to play the game, which was what caused my stress in life. So, my favorite game became the supermarket game. Before I knew how to play this game, I would take my child to the supermarket, and I would just automatically expect her to behave with my other two. I would automatically think that they would want nothing in the supermarket except for what I bought. I would automatically think that if I told them, then they would know that they wouldn't just get it, and they would not argue with me. I would think that they could actually resist, as a child, all the marketing tricks of the trade.

Luckily (I don't know where I read it, but it works like a charm), I read that your children will never starve themselves, and they will eat what is easy to access. Now my children prefer fruits and vegetables as snacks over anything else because, when they were young, I would cut up and peel all fruits and vegetables, and place them in the fridge at their eye level. So, when they were hungry, they would see carrots cut up, watermelon, etc. I mean, we lived in Jamaica, so fresh fruits and vegetables were in abundance, and they loved it. I also grew what we ate, and ate what we grew, by going into organic farming. Because I read that pesticides encouraged autism, I started farming, and the kids loved the fresh vegetables that I grew on the farm, so they would actually eat straight from the farm as well. However, in Jamaica, fruits from America were extremely expensive, but my children loved grapes and strawberries, and they loved the short carrot things, which were very expensive, and I could not afford them. My child would have temper tantrums, and I would panic. Later, I realized that all she was doing was communicating to me without using words. She was saying, "I am tired, I am hungry, and I want to go home." She also communicated without words and used a temper tantrum when I told her that she could not have bubble gum, or that she could not have grapes or anything else she wanted, because how could she understand, at age three and four, that I could not afford it.

Having a child with autism, the therapy is more for the parents than for the child. I was taught how to understand her, and that with ANY GAME , we never play without learning the rules of the game first, so I communicated the rules of the game before I went into the supermarket: "McKenzie, Benjamin, and Christopher, I can only buy what's on the list." I read out the list to them, and I asked them to help me find the items on the list. I explained to them that we have just enough money to afford what's on the list; however, if there was any money left over, they could have one treat each, under a certain amount of money. This game that I played (because they treated it like a game) was, "Let's go find items on the list for Mommy, and let's learn about money." I love helping them to find items of their choice under a certain amount of money. After this game was established, I had 100% success in the supermarket—no tantrums.

As they grew older, the rules had to change as well. They were no longer interested in finding out what was on the list, because they had learned the tricks of that game—the same way that they got bored of Candyland, and you had to move on to Monopoly. So, now that they are older, instead of me communicating the list and asking them to find a few things, I now give them the list, and it is now their turn to do the shopping, but here is the game: "I spent x amount of dollars last week; try and beat my price by lowering the bill. If you spend less than I did last week, you'll receive a prize."

What did this game do? The first thing is that it helped them to work together, something that was not happening at that time because they were all clashing with each other. So now they were working together to beat Mommy and her list—they were looking at the prices, they were looking at different types of products, and they actually would beat me in pricing (even though there were certain brand names that I prefer to use in the house). What I did was to give them the credit back in their bank account. So, what I have learnt is that you can use games, and recycle the games at every age of their lives; however, make it more difficult, and respect that they're getting older and that they're not always going to be young children. Your way of communicating with your children changes over time, and so does the game.

I have lots of life games on my website, but I hope you can think of your own. I know that the parents in my online course have told me how much they appreciate these little games, and how to communicate the games; and in my workshops, parents have come back to say that setting the rules beforehand alleviates a lot of the temper tantrums at the younger ages, and the arguments at the older ages. Children want to know where they stand. They like routine and rules; it actually makes them feel safe.

In the next chapter, I speak about getting to know our children and even ourselves. I had to get to know my three children and how they have their own perceptions. They not only have their own experiences but their own (how they watch their elders, meaning their daddy and me, and how we behave in scenarios). So, for example, I had an abusive marriage, where my husband would shout at me every night, be verbally abusive to me and tell me bad things about myself. So, how can I turn around and punish my son for doing the same thing to my daughter when he is angry about having a bad day, or annoyed with her (which was compounded by the fact that she got more attention from me at the time, because of her autism). Experience is gained from what they learn and see, more than from what they have experienced themselves. Just like their father, they would take out their bad day on the people they loved. I had to observe this game, and realized that it needed changing.

I had to appreciate that my children are three completely different individuals, because they witnessed this abuse that they saw their mother go through, at different ages in their lives. My oldest protected my little ones from hearing it, so they could not understand the anger that my oldest had toward their father. However, later in time, as they got older the two younger ones started to understand what their brother was saying, they got the blame, when they started withdrawing from their father and that hurt them more than him because children have unconditional love for their parents. We have to be absolutely awful as a parent for our children to stop loving us. Even the worse parents still receive some hope from the children that they will love them one day. This is a big responsibility because that unconditional love should be respected, nurtured, and rewarded. We are the adults and should always take the higher road and turn all bad moments into teaching moments but an argument about who is right or wrong. Dig deeper and ask questions when your child is doing something you think is wrong.

What helped me to realize this was the fact that all my children struggled in school, and needed psychological and educational testing at early ages due to their dyslexia and autism. This helped the schools and myself to get to know their individual educational plan (IEP) well. I look at parenting the same way as I look at teaching, so I developed their IDP (individual development plan) and their IPP (individual personality plan). Take into account that it evolves and needs reassessing yearly, and sometimes monthly. You can get my examples on my website. My children have learning exceptionalities, and their teachers had learning disabilities, because their teachers did not know how to teach them. I'm just like that. I had to learn to teach them and help them through school with this information that I had about how they learn. I also took this information on how they think, and that's how I taught them in life as a parent.

I even developed some great family games, called The Hot Seat, and The Guess Who Game, to encourage family members on game night to get to know each other. You, as the parent, can even learn, in a respectful way, what your children think of you. Help them to know what you think of them, and what they think of each other, in a positive way. Most times, we talk about our children when we're angry or disciplining them, which is in the negative way, but if we can help understand each other, and open that line of communication in a positive, fun way again, you're changing it from hostility to harmony.

On my radio show in Jamaica, I didn't just talk about parenting; I advocated for the children of Jamaica. Jamaica still has a society where parents punish and beat their children. We are a society that still believes that if you spare the rod, you spoil the child. We did not know the difference between discipline and punishment. The saying, "Sticks and stones will break my bones but words will never hurt me," was taught to all victims of bullying, and the same victims would have to change schools if they could not handle the verbal abuse. Well, I have learnt otherwise, and I am grateful for my marriage and the experience. I am grateful that I was able to recover and help my children to recover. Through this experience, from marriage to separation and divorce, I was able to develop a new game and new rules, to teach my children compassion, love, and forgiveness. Their unconditional love for their father and me caused me to have to consider their perspective when teaching the divorce game to them.

So, even though I teach my children to play the game, I guess it's also right to say that they have taught me just as much through their lessons—I understand how to actively listen to them. The last thing our children want to do is disappoint us or hurt us, or make us angry, so they make genuine mistakes, and instead of punishing these mistakes, we should always dig deeper to find out why the mistake was made. We can help them to learn that it was a mistake, and to learn the consequences of the mistake—and that, my fellow parents, is called discipline.

My village is so important to me. This includes my children's teachers, and their father, that I am no longer with, as well as my family, their coaches, their doctors, and my best friend, Maria, and her kids. Whenever I add somebody to the village, I have to let them know the game and the rules of my child, especially the biggest parent partners I have, which are the teachers. Many times, we don't give enough information to our teachers, sometimes because we don't want them to know our personal lives and what's happening within those; and that's not fair, not just to the teachers but to the children as well.

So, when I moved to Canada, I actually moved to Canada for my children. They were being bullied at school. My daughter was being bullied by her peers, and my son was being bullied by his teacher; and he would have had that teacher next year. We were also not handling the divorce well, and every other weekend with their dad was difficult, as they were hearing bad things about me. Their dad wasn't dealing with what happened, but that's a whole different book. So, when I met the teachers for the first year, in Canada, I sat down and told them the whole story of what my children were going through. I gave them their psycho-educational reports, and I told them where they were academically and mentally, health-wise.

If my children had a meltdown or were upset the night before, I would email the teachers and let them know. When we don't play the school game really well, our children can fall through the cracks; or worse, they could be treated in the wrong way, which would make their emotional state worse. Never have I had a teacher tell me that I'm giving them too much information; in fact, they embrace it and thank me for being such a proactive parent, and for giving them a heads-up on how the children are. This goes for their education as well. Even though my children are in high school, university, and elementary, I'm very proactive with them, and I know where they stand and what they do at school at all times—they know the rules.

One thing I did that I found works was to actually be a part of the school councils, PTA, and anything that supports the school. When you are a supportive parent, the school becomes very supportive of your child. It's just the way the game works, and the side benefit that I learned from my oldest son is that when he knows you're at school, and you're part of the school, the teachers find it very easy to talk to you. So he can't get away with as much as he thought he could, because he knows that if he doesn't do his homework, the teachers will see me in the halls, or they'll see me around, and they will tell me very quickly. So, he knows, and all three of them now know that they can't get away with anything, because the communication is constant between their teachers and myself.

My co-host, Phil Edwards, on my YouTube parenting show, Interpersonal Parenting, talks about having a caring adult in your village. We'll explore it in future chapters, about personalities of our children and of ourselves, and how they are different and yet similar, and how they will clash and how they will mesh. This is where your caring adult in the village is so important. The caring adult is the one person that your child can go to as a sounding board and advisor; and a lot of times, it's a sounding board to say, "Hey, how do you think Mom and Dad will react?"

I have to confess that when he mentioned it in the show, my eyes opened wide, because I used to be jealous of caring adults in my village. I thought that if my children went to them and not me, then I was doing something wrong; however, in the show, when we discussed it, it really came down to personalities. And I had to learn that my children don't always know how to communicate with me, and that it doesn't mean that I am a bad parent. It could be just that they don't want to disappoint me, or that they think they're disappointing me and, therefore, they don't want to approach me with it. They may even go to my sister or my brother, or somebody else that knows me really well, to sound off to them. If they don't know what to say about what is occurring, they would suggest that they go to their mom about it, and then they would come to me.

Here, I'd like to thank my sister, Lynda, who has been a caring adult for my oldest son, Christopher; and yes, I was very jealous at first, but thanks to my Interpersonal Parenting co-coach, Phil and the show we did on parenting during the summer, I now appreciate who she is. I guess part of the jealousy came about from that triangle and my sibling issues. I know that I've learned through communication how to handle everything, and I'm no longer jealous. Many times, the family game that we played as young kids carries over to the next generation.

The game never changes; however, the rules can. Remember, we're not just parents; we're also human beings, and we evolve. I mean, what is a midlife crisis but us changing our games as adults. The rules can change, and I think we need to definitely communicate to our children that this can happen to them. We can't expect our children to apologize and change if they do not see us apologize for our mistakes as people and parents, to ensure that we can change as well. When I make a mistake, especially with my kids, I immediately apologize. I say, "Hey guys, I made a mistake. Mommy's a little on edge right now, and I didn't mean to shout. I'm sorry; I'll try not to do it again." And I'm going to touch on the blame game right now, because we always tend to fall into that trap.

How many times do we blame our children for pestering us and annoying us. Do you say things in an aggressive tone like, "Do you have to attack me as I get home? ", "Can you give me a break for five minutes?", "Why do you not have the house clean and your chores done when I get home?" When you come home from work, and you're tired and you're frustrated, your kids don't see or know what you did at work or what's up at work. They're just so happy to see you and to actually tell you about their day, and they ask for things that they need because they have waited all day to see you. They don't realize that we need our peace and quiet too. We're there for them, so this rule can evolve, where you say, "Okay, I understand that I'm there for you, but Mommy (or Daddy) is very tired when I come home from work. Can you give me 5 minutes to just put my bags down, and then I'll talk to you?" Or if you don't want them to wait, one of the exercises I actually do is a dragon's breath, of which I will post a video on my website. In fact, a lot of these games and things are in my Interpersonal Parenting online course, and there are videos and explanations of them, which is really cool with the templates of some of the games that we play.

Stay in your car for 5 minutes before you go inside, and relax and chill, and then go inside when you're ready to face the kids. That does not change the rules that you have established, and it does not change the minute they see you at the end of the day. When you walk through that door, they're going to need you, so you now have to change your strategy. If you cannot handle it, maybe you can even go to the gym right after work before you go home. There's nothing wrong with that; as long as you're there to put them to bed, and they see you before they go to sleep, there's nothing wrong. Self-care is a rule that we must never change in the game. I learned that so late in life, and I have to admit that this was my mother. She never did any self-care. She taught me that I must sacrifice everything for my children, and that I must never have any time for myself. It must all be for your children and your husband—and she suffered from depression. It wasn't until I reached my lowest of lows as a woman that I realized I needed self-care. So when that rule changed in the game, and Mommy was going to have self-care time, I became a better parent, to the point where none of my kids had to tell me that I needed my self-care (which was our code word to tell me that I was not handling something really well), or that I was in a miserable mood and needed to have some self-care.

Again, our children have that unconditional love where they want to see us happy as much as we want to see them happy. And we can hide our own happiness as much as we think we can, but they, especially because they were in our bodies at one time, feel what we feel, and it's unbelievable how that connection happens even after birth; so that hiding of emotions game doesn't work with children— they feel what we feel. Rules can also change with divorce. The whole dynamic of the family changes when that happens, and I want to thank my lawyer, Chris Dunkley, for teaching me that in divorce everybody loses. The only win you aim for is that children don't lose. I've seen innovative ways to help children transition with divorce, and one is to let the kids keep the house, where the parents are the ones who move in and out. It's a great idea, and I thought it was wonderful.

That's a tidbit, however. Let's go back to the rules changing when a separation or divorce happens. Let's sit down and think of the new rules, and establish them between both parents, because you're still parent partners; and yes, you have unresolved issues between yourselves, and you have a lot of anger and hurt. That's why immediately sitting down and establishing the rules for the children is so important. It takes the emotion out of it when it's on a piece of paper, and you know if you have that open communication with your family already, including the kids. You can sit them down and tell them, "Hey, Mommy and Daddy are getting a divorce. What would you like to see happen with this?" Include them in the decision making; that is probably one of the most healing games you can play when it comes to this big rule change.

Chapter 3

GAME OF GUESS WHO

Now it is time to play some games! In order to communicate effectively, we need to know our receivers of information, and not to think that we know them because we gave birth to them. The key is to be aware that we do not know them! Huh? Yes, appreciating that you actually do not know how your children think, or who they are, is the best way to communicate with them. But you have to be careful at the same time not to patronize them.

So, there are four ways that we actually view and function as ourselves, so I'm going to work on this before I tell you how to work on yourself. I mention this in the next chapter, about the Time to Shine, My Words Are Mine game, and this is a great presentation skill that we're teaching our kids. To explain, we make a presentation on ourselves, and we have to save four categories. Now, when you have toddlers or young children that speak, you know that if you're finding issues with them, they learn from examples. The older ones will also learn from you, and they'll learn from their older siblings. So, the information in the Time to Shine, My Words Are Mine is all about self-concept and, therefore, categories that they have to look at, and where they have to gather information. Most times, it is a reflection.

The first one is what others think of you, and others are people that are important in your life. So, when I did my self-concept exercise, I actually asked people that I had a relationship with: my best friend, my sister, my brother, my mother, and my significant other. I did this section last, because I'm a person that will listen to what other people think, versus how I think about myself, and I did not want it all to be about how I felt about myself. The second one is the comparison with others (how I compare to others that I know), and it doesn't have to be a significant other this time. You look at the outside to see how you compare to your peers. How do you compare to people at work; how do you compare to people in your social group; how do you compare to people your age and situation?

Then we look at self-evaluations. How do you evaluate your feelings and behaviors? This self-evaluation should actually be done on how you feel and why. It's based on what others think of you, as well as how you compare yourself to others. It really is a self-evaluation on how you treat life. Then the final category, before we even reach self-concept, is cultural teachings. Cultural teaching is how you reflect on how you fulfill your cultural teachings, meaning not just how you practice your religion or how you behave toward other people, or your norms that you have learnt in your culture, but also how you go establishing your authentic self and your children's when you do not believe in something things in your culture or maybe everything? So, for example, in my cultural teachings, my behavior and beliefs always went against what I was taught. I'm a Jamaican, born and bred, and an 8th generation Jamaican; however, I'm also a white Jamaican. A minority site considered me white with a black culture because I embraced Mike Scott's Jamaican culture and believed in our quotation, "Out of many, 1 people." I'm a born Jewess but grew up as a Christian. I was born in a certain class in Jamaica, but I belong to all classes. I don't believe in class, and I'm white, with a Jamaican accent and culture, and live in Canada. So I even go against my mirror existence, and the cultural teachings that I have been taught, and I love it, appreciate it, and embrace it. This is why, in the online course, Interpersonal Parenting, this is one of the first exercises we give the family to do, and we make it a game called Time to Shine, My Words Are Mine.

So now I'm going to pay homage to yet another author that I absolutely love. It's called, *Raise the Child You've Got—Not the One You Want*, by Nancy Rose. If you go on the website above, you can actually get a special discount for her book, because it's one of my resources that have helped me through life. In the next chapter, Mirror Me, Mirror You, you'll read about how I learnt the hard way to raise a child I have, and not the one I want. Knowing the child you have is not that easy, because our children evolve over time. However, I'm going to give you yet another template, and this one is for free on my website, and it's a little test to help you learn or to help you decipher how your children learn. No, I did the expensive route, because my three children have dyslexia, and my daughter has autism. I actually went through the cycle of educational reports, and paid lots of money for them, but I learned so much from these reports, and believe it or not, these reports helped me parent my children in a harmonious way. They gave me the tools to learn about the child I had, and it helped me to develop their strengths and improve their weaknesses.

I love these types of templates and tests, and you can make it fun and age appropriate to help you decipher how your children are and how they learn. What I love about the one that we have in the online course is that it actually helps you identify the characteristic skills, as opposed to the learning type. I'll give you a quick example. I'm verbal and the greatest linguistic; I have interpersonal intelligence and musical intelligence, but I have spatial disabilities and visual disabilities in the sense that I have to measure everything. Don't ask me to decorate your room or fit anything in a space—math is not my strong point. When I did the test, and I learned that I had interpersonal intelligence, it meant that I have the ability to really relate to people and notice their moods and motivations. I feel them. I'm an empath, and I guess that's what gave me the advantage to observe people and my family, and how we are. Hence, it is why I'm writing this book, to hopefully help you. I really encourage you to take the test first, and find out who you are before you unleash this and tell everybody else, because if you don't have that interpersonal intelligence, then you have to be aware of it. But hey, what I love about it as well is that everybody has their own skills, so one of your children might have interpersonal intelligence, but you have mathematical; so therefore, you can help them mathematically, while they can help you with interpersonal intelligence. Of course, with my interpersonal intelligence, I also have verbal linguistic intelligence, meaning that I have the ability to communicate through language, listening, and reading, as well as the fact that I can pick up tones and voices, which is also musical intelligence. So, I can hear nonverbal cues, and see nonverbal cues easily. Sometimes it can be confusing because people say something different to how they're actually feeling or how their tone or body language is, so this intelligence, and being high in this intelligence, can be a disadvantage as well as an advantage. The advantages are that I'm able to write this book and produce the online courses to help other people. I really hope that you go on the website to get the bonus and download the test, and have fun with your family, and find out whom they really are.

So, what is the other side, when you don't accept the child you have, or you don't know the child you have or have the child you think you have? Well, I'm going back to my childhood, I played a certain role of who I was to my family but my authentic self was so different. I spent my life feeling unaccepted and lost. As a parent we can also do this to our children. Who your children are in front of you, and who they are behind your back or when you're not around, are two different people, and sometimes that's not a good thing. What you are trying to achieve is for your child to be their authentic self at all times.

When I was growing up, I could relate back to the cultural teaching and how defiant I was to them leading to this. Thankfully, I had a safe and nurturing environment to realize my authentic self, called the Little People and Teen Players Club Performing Arts Company. Here, I was my true self; in other words, how my theatre family perceived me as an actress—an easy going, non-judgemental, loving person—was the identity I wanted. However, I had my mother's perception of me that I must act like I belong to a certain class of upper-society Jamaicans. I was constantly insulted when I would let my inner Jamaican come out, and was always encouraged to marry an upper society Jamaican man. This caused me to have a negative self-identity, because I did not behave or think the way I should. I always felt less than, unworthy, and an outcast in my family. So I would always use image-confirming strategies to avoid being reprimanded, meaning that I would portray who they wanted me to be, and I actually ended up falling in love and marrying the right man, and getting a divorce.

So, you see how important it is that we encourage our children to be their own authentic self with us at all times so that we can truly get them. If they are using that self-imaging in front of you, then you're actually not guiding them in the right way. I was especially not doing this recently with my child who has autism. And I'm going to explain the biggest parenting mistake I believe I made. When I discovered that my daughter had autism, 10 years ago, we searched how to take her off the spectrum. In the research that I did, I was told that it could happen if you didn't feed them vegetables with pesticides, and if they had no gluten and had behavior modification. We did everything, including teaching her how to articulate using her words. I forced my child to look me in the eye the minute I found out, and that's why she couldn't look me in the eye. I grew organic vegetables and fed them to her, which she loves, so I'm really happy about that. The behavioral modification (I call it the star chart) worked like a charm, not just for my daughter but also for my boys as well, so I highly recommend that. Again, that is just communication. You take one behavior you would like to change in each child, put it on a calendar, and every day that they don't do that behavior, they get a star. Again, the template is on the website, and I'm definitely giving it to you as a free bonus, because it was my biggest tool to help my children, especially when they were younger, as they couldn't do these games. That's the best way to modify their social behavior—temper tantrums, crying excessively, biting, kicking, not doing their homework or things that they need to do—and it's positive reinforcement and communicating, and taking out the stress and fighting in order to change behaviors.

My daughter and I had a rough time in the beginning, schools were kicking her out because her behavior, and she was being bullied at school for her differences; and instead of me celebrating her differences and telling her to be confident with them, I told her not to be different. Fast-forward 10 years, and she's a beautiful teenager, almost the perfect child. Her room is clean, and she gets up every morning and goes to school. She does have certain things that I constantly have to work with her about, but she depends on me and trusts me impeccably, to the point where I'm the only person she depends on and trusts. She does her homework but not always on time, because she does not have an appreciation for time, she freezes when everything is due or worse if she doesn't know how to do something, she shuts down and doesn't do it at all. Then has an anxiety attack, uses self-deprivation words and a meltdown if she doesn't do well. She has a noise issue, so she constantly worries about the noise. Loud noises hurt her, but she hid all of that from me. By me bragging that she had been taken off the spectrum, she began to create the self-image I was bragging about—the perfect child, the perfect teenager. But all this time, her authentic, beautiful, autistic self was hidden away from me, and I truly could not help her. So when she had a meltdown out of the blue, whether at school or at home, I wondered why this was happening, because I believed that she was off the spectrum. But she was not; she was hiding it until the weight of her self-image became so heavy that she would break and have a meltdown.

I knew something was wrong (again, going back to my intelligences and being an empath), and I knew that Canada would be the best country for her. The minute we got off the plane and she started going to school, she started showing, over months, signs of her autism. I wondered if I had done the right thing, coming to Canada. I actually thought that she had gotten worse, not better. I started going to workshops for autism because I wanted to get her off the spectrum again. I then learnt that you can never take them off the spectrum, and every day I came home from a workshop, and I learnt something more about autism and autistic children. No one is the same. I would go to her and say, "McKenzie, is this how you feel?" She would look at me with the brightest eyes, saying with her eyes, "Well, Mommy, you see me now," and I started appreciating who she really was, and I was then able to guide her authentic self. What I learnt now was her self-damaging talk, her lack of self-confidence, and her non-aggressive behavior, and I saw a light that was actually dying in her. She was completely self-imaging to me and I was doing to her what my mother did to me.

I've had to personally go through a lot of self-care and reflection since my divorce and didn't even know that I was self-imaging my marriage to everybody and not showing my authentic self. In fact, my self-image became my authentic self. I find that a lot of women do that, and then we don't know why we're unhappy.

So, here's a new game: 10 Things I Love About You. I offer this program in my parent coaching courses, but I'll give you a gist of what it is. I teach parents the game where they have to write 10 things that they love about their children, and then they have to tell them this. In turn, they have to write 10 things that they love about themselves. And then I offer the exercises of letter writing. I mean, we all have letter writing, and I write letters to myself every birthday, and I do it specifically on a birthday because I believe that we can be reborn and evolve every year of our lives, and it has been very rewarding.

I now do that for my children, and we write it in a birthday card; but this is a letter, and I know that the postal system in Canada is so much better than in Jamaica, so I write the letter, and I post it to them. So, on their birthday, they get a posted letter in the mail from me, wishing them a happy birthday and telling them things that I love about them, and things that I'd like to see improve in them this year.

And a lot of that improvement is encouraging them to see what they need to improve themselves, so I don't identify what they need to improve—I encourage them to improve what they want to improve. In return, I get them to write 10 things that they love about themselves, and 10 things they love about me. There is a lot of love in a harmonious family; we see that love every day, and we show that love every day. A parent's love is free; there is no charge, and the greatest gift we can give our children is to say that we love them every day, and to show them that we love them every day, giving them that sense of belonging and that they know they have a place to be safe in, to be loved in, and to be celebrated. The world is harsh and ready to pull you down, but if they know they have one place to go where they feel safe from the world, they will be happy.

A second game I play, every day of my life or whenever the children are giving me some reasons to make me angry, or they are trying to get out of doing something or they're unhappy, is that I always dig deeper. Again, I benefit from being an empath, so they may say, "Mom, everything is fine. I'm great; the day was great," but in their tone, I would hear something completely different. I would say to them "You know, why didn't you do the dishes tonight? Your chore is supposed to be doing the dishes. That is your schedule and your responsibility. You know what you need to do. I shouldn't have to come and tell you." And if they get angry at me, I dig deeper. Whenever they have a bad response, I dig deeper, and they know this is coming now. They'll get angry or they'll have an outburst, or the fighting will start, but it takes two people to fight, so if they're angry at me or they snap back at me, I say, "Hold on there. Why are you angry? Why are you acting like this?" And they say, "Mom, you're going to dig deeper, aren't you?" And I say, "Yes, I am.

In my parent coaching workshops, I do exercises to help dig deeper. Digging deeper is gathering information, instead of making statements about why the child is behaving that way. I had a teacher tell me this and encourage me to do it in my interview in class. In fact, it was very impactful in my life. I used to be that parent where I would accuse, and I would try and solve things immediately, and I would go into solution mode the minute everybody was in a bad mood—again, being the avoider, trying to avoid the conflict, trying to avoid the fight, instead of dealing with the root cause of the problem. So, when I actually took a class on interviewing, because I was studying to be a social worker, the techniques used in the class were incredibly helpful with dealing with this situation.

When my child was having conflict, anger, or bad behavior, for which I was trying to figure out why, I dug deeper, using my interviewing skills and my communication skills, and I stopped making statements and solutions, and started asking the questions. In order to do this and to be effective in gathering information, even though they may say their day was fine, ask why it was fine. Ask if there is a reason that they sound so angry, and be aware when they don't want to tell you. It could be the environment. Sometimes my children would call me when they're out, and they would say that they want to come home. Well, yes, I'm going to say that I'm going to go get them, but I ask them why they want to come home. "I just want to come home, okay?" is the answer. "Will you tell me why you want to come home when you get in the car and we're alone?" I ask. "Yes, Mommy, okay." So, I have diffused the situation or deescalated the situation on that angle, because they already know that they're going to tell me when they get in the car, so they won't be as angry when I pick them up.

Remember, digging deeper is gathering information: Why are you behaving this way now? Even that question is very statement oriented, so it's more like how you are feeling right now: Are you angry? Are you sad? Are you tired? Even though my daughter is 15, I constantly have to ask these questions and teach her these feelings, as much as find out what the feeling is. I look at the nonverbal communication, which I'll go into later on in another chapter, but the key components for digging deeper are, believe it or not, self-awareness, empathy, and genuineness. You have to genuinely want to know why they are behaving that way, not just to solve the problem and to stop them from behaving that way. You have to respect them and offer your opinion, and not be defensive, because sometimes, believe it or not, you are the cause of the problem! It's very, very important to not show approval or disapproval; just be very neutral in what you're saying, because what you're trying to do is gather information by asking open-ended questions. Don't ask questions where you're going to get one-word answers. Instead, ask what they did today, or what their favorite thing was that they did today. Ask what they didn't like doing today.

And when you're trying to get more of the story out of them, use encouraging words. For example, your child is telling you about how they had a conflict with a friend at school, or kids at school are changing friends, which happens in middle school. The friends you start with sometimes are not the friends that you end up with at the end of the year, because you're evolving, and you're all going through puberty. All that adds up when I'm trying to get the information, and it can happen where they have a bad day at school, because we can have a bad day at work, and we come home in a miserable mood. Well, when your child has a bad day at school, they come home in a miserable mood. So let's handle this scenario.

For example, I need to find out why my son is in a bad mood and is picking on his sister, so I'll ask what happened at school today. If he replies that nothing happened, then I need to find a way to build rapport with him. I cannot be judgmental, and I cannot say that I know something's wrong, but it's really hard for me not to say that I know something's wrong. But I show empathy, and eventually, with the encouraging words and asking how his friend is today (I don't know whether something's up with his friend because they usually talk every day), I dig deeper, and then I hear that they're not talking to him right now. I would ask him how he handled that, and how he felt about it. After he explains how he handled it, I would say that I think he handled it very well, and I would ask what else he did to handle the situation.

Your body language is also very important when you're trying to get information out of your children. Don't cross your arms, and your tone must be gentle and soft and non-judgmental. Sit down and relax, and make sure that your environment is not going to enable them to get really anxious or angry, and if that happens, then you have to know how to deescalate by removing yourself. Tell them that you know they are getting upset right now, and suggest that you stop talking for a bit and have something to drink. Make them feel that you're interested in what they're saying, and make sure that it's one on one. Then you can go into the goal setting. Ask how they want to handle the situation. Ask if they really like being around these kids. Don't push your solution on them. You can suggest a solution, and if they like it, they can take it; if they don't like it, then leave it alone.

So, again, the key to these games, these solutions, are all in my online course, and I do them in my parenting workshop. You'll see some of the templates on the free bonuses page on my website for the book. Use them and enjoy them. You will get to know your child because we have many more games to come in this book. In the next chapter, I talk about the Chore game and how we handle one big scenario that is constant in my house, and which causes issues, and how it is now harmonious versus stressful for me.

What I truly hope that you get from this chapter, and what I have gotten from it, is that you learn just as much about yourself as you do about your children. We also learn that we evolve and we change, and that every year is a year of growth and rebirth, and even the bad things in life that happened to you are good things in life when it comes to learning from them. So, let's start playing some games.

Chapter 4

THE CHORE GAME

This is a three-player game. Now, I have three players in this game. I have myself (again, I'm interpersonal, and I'm an empath), I have my daughter (who is self- imaging in every way right now), and then I have my youngest son (who is benefiting from all the self-reflection and education that I've been going through, and it's funny how he's learning just as much as I am, because he too is very good at verbal intelligence and interpersonal intelligence). So, who is my challenge to get them to do what I want them to do in this game? Not my daughter who is self- imaging—she's going to do everything, and all she wants to do is to please me. She does her chores exactly when she is supposed to do them, and how she is supposed to do them. If she does not want to do them, she tells me that she is very tired and that she doesn't want to do them. I think if I ask them the same thing, and explain that at times I am tired, why can't I accept that from them? However, even though I accept that reason, I also ensure that we agree on another time to get the chore done.

But my son, who now does not like to clean his room or public areas in the house, and always wants help to do his chores, which is taking out the garbage and the recycling every night, is more of a challenge. But I do have a disclaimer for him: We come from Jamaica where we have people to do this for us. We don't have recycling in Jamaica, and the garbage is once a week. It goes out, and it stays outside and it's collected. We have these containers at the foot of the driveway, so once you put it out, you don't have to take it to the front and put it in the back, and it's a lot less trouble. So it was very new for my children to even do laundry, or clean the house themselves, do dishes, or just general housework.

Now that I've given you the background of my players, letting you know who they are, and what they're capable of at this point in time, how do you think I should play the chore game? If you answered that when I tell two of my children to go clean their room, in the same tone and using the same words, it is guaranteed that I will get two different reactions, you are right, because they are two different people. My daughter will go immediately, but my son will argue and say that he does not need to do it now. Now, should I argue with my son, and tell him that he should be more like his sister, or do I step back, stop forcing my son to make my life easier, and communicate how he listens? So, I rewind and tell my daughter to clean her room, and she goes. Then I turn to my son, using a tool called Jhari's window. This theory explains how every conversation goes between sender and receiver.

My son and I both have open thoughts, hidden thoughts, blind thoughts, and unknown thoughts. So let's use my cleaning room example with my twelve-year- old son, Benjamin. Benjamin and I are aware that I am going to ask him to clean his room, because I just asked his sister to do it. Benjamin's hidden thought (or so he thinks) is that he would rather not clean his room but do something else. Another hidden thought is that he is hiding something in his room. Let's take the first theory. My hidden thought is that I already know he doesn't want to clean his room, and I also know that he loves to go play Magic the Gathering on Friday nights (it is Thursday). So I am already prepared for negotiation, because that is what he loves to do. Benjamin is my negotiator and leader in the family. He has cerebral talents. So here is the tricky part: In every conversation, there is an unknown factor, unknown to both Benjamin and me. This is what you have to expect every time, and react accordingly.

So, let's go back to the scenario. I approach Benjamin, and I tell him that if he does not clean his room or do what I ask, should I do what he asks by taking him to the card shop on Friday to play his favourite game? He stops and thinks. Here is the unknown: There might not be a tournament or a game on Friday. See how I worded it? I did not threaten or bribe him; I made him think about how we interact with each other. By using what I know, by considering what he is hiding from me, and what I do not know that he is hiding from me, and even if there is a game on Friday, by changing the way I spoke to him, I pushed him to use the same thought process. He then applies the same theory: I know Mum wants me to clean my room. I do not want to clean my room. I want to play on my computer, but will she not take me Friday? I do not want to take a chance; let me go clean my room. I actually leave the question open ended as well. Hopefully, he will think that the next time he asks me for anything, I will not do it because he did not do this, so if the tournament is not on, I have another chance to say no to him.

We should never use these instances as conflicts, which I'll go into more in the chapter on scenarios. What we need to do is consider it a negotiation, which actually can be fine. In fact, I studied negotiation and I loved it, so I sit down with my fellow mind, meaning my son who is like me (remember, interpersonal intelligence and verbal and linguistic), and I say, "Let the negotiations begin." Sometimes we don't have a chance, and sometimes we don't have the time, or we're tired; however, what would you rather do—enter into a negotiation with your son, or have an argument? How many times do we as a parent actually start the argument because we just don't have time? We're on our phones, or we had a bad day at work... there are so many reasons that we just had to get it done. Because, guess what, our kids are the easiest people to take out our anger on, because they're there, and we know that they love us at any time, no matter what we do. But is that really the right approach?

Sometimes we win the negotiation, and sometimes we don't win the negotiation, but what we try and aim to do is that both he and I win. In other words, that is where we always aim to be. I listen to his reason why he doesn't clean his room, or it'll end up where we both wait till his room is so messy, because I can shut the door on that one; however, the common areas, where I have to live and I have to be in, I don't want to see his things, and it must be clean, and he agrees to that. The key to every game, when it comes to identifying and reducing the fighting and the stress, is making sure that both parties win, and both parties get what they want out of it. Again, I'll explain this more in another chapter, but I just gave you a little taste of how I handle one example on how I play the game with my children.

I actually have these techniques and tips in my parenting workshops, and we go through scenarios. That's why I love the parenting workshops, because the parents actually tell me the main issues in their home. We are able to work through it together, and I can give them the negotiation stance on it, and the parents love it. They always come back with a smiling face the next day, and they say, "Hey, I actually tackled it with no arguments, and we both got what we wanted."

Usually, in these instances, as well as seeing me, I see their dad, and I see other influences in their life, and this leads me to my next chapter about how we see our children, how they see us, and how they can make us not only better parents but also better people.

Chapter 5

MIRROR ME, MIRROR YOU

Has your child or any child slapped you? When it happened to me, my first thought was, how dare they slap me. Then I really thought about it. Hold on, I just slapped them for being bad, and they just thought I was bad. They are just mirroring our actions, so do we punish them and leave it at that, or do we teach them, and in so doing, change our behavior as well?

However, I think it goes deeper than that. If we are our children's mirrors, then they can be our mirrors too, if you can truly accept that your children can teach you. Can you imagine the person you could be if you could mirror their pure and true qualities? However, in order to do this, we truly have to know who our children are. I said it before, and I'll say it again: My children came out of the same place but have three completely different personalities. If we want our children to be treated as an individual in school and in life, we should treat them as individuals as well. We identify their positive qualities and praise them, and identify their negative qualities and help them learn to change them. In my online course, I offer a behavioral modification technique that I used with my daughter who has autism, but the benefits that I saw with my two boys were incredible. I'd like to thank her psychologists, Dr. Rose Johnson and Dr. Tracy Coley, who gave me those tools in Jamaica, and helped me so much with behavioral modification for my daughter. At the time, I thought I had brought her off the spectrum, but now I realize there's no doing that, even though her behavior has changed. She went from having a temper tantrum a day, and screaming for an hour straight, to not screaming at all. In fact, now, at 15 years old, she is actually my best-behaved child, and the behaviors I need to help her with are using positive language for herself and being more social.

Going back to our children being our teachers, this has come to be a strong belief of mine as a parent. Not only do the children feel pride when they teach me something (and it's not just technology; it is the good qualities that they have inherited or learned, or just genetics that have composed into a beautiful symphony), I feel the pride that they have, and that is a positive quality that I can learn from. This has created such a great relationship with my children. They can respectfully tell me how they feel, and I don't feel offended, and if I do, I just say, "Hey, I feel offended with what you said. Can you say it a little better?" Then the atmosphere in the household definitely moves from hostile to harmony.

I am now going to share with you three important qualities I have seen in my children, which I try to mirror each day.

- The first quality is to accept people for who they are and not for who you want them to be.
- The second quality is the value of the power of kind words.
- The third quality is to always keep your promises, or don't make them in the first place.

The first quality I try to mirror is the one taught by my eldest son, Christopher, who showed me the quality of accepting people for who they are and not what we want them to be.

Christopher is a natural athlete.

1. At 10, he was scouted for three national teams—squash, golf, and table tennis.

2. At 12, he won a scholarship to Valencia Spain for football, and played for the U15 team for Waterhouse Club.

I immediately saw him walking behind our Jamaican flag proudly representing our country at the Olympics.

So, you can imagine the disappointment I felt when I went to my son and asked what sport he wanted to pursue, and the details of working for greatness, and his reply was, "I don't like to compete; I just like to play!"

But I kept pushing, and all it caused was constant fights between my son and me, which led to him constantly feeling that he was not good enough.

I was trying to parent the child I wanted, a child with a strong competitive drive—my Olympian—not the child who is naturally relaxed, reserved, and strategic.

So I started to appreciate him and support him on his dreams, and he has grown into a confident and happy young man that I am proud to call my son.

Remember to appreciate people for who they are and not who you want them to be.

The second quality I try to mirror is from my second child, my daughter, Mckenzie. She taught me the power of kind words. When I look at her, I see more of me—but the younger me—the Rebecca I used to be before my experiences hardened me.

Her reflection teaches me to appreciate the power of using kind words, and how good that makes others feel. She appreciates every moment, and the people that love and care for her.

- She demonstrates one of my favourite Maya Angelou quotes: "I've learned that people will forget what you said, people will forget what you did, but people will never forget how you made them feel."
- When she gets out of the car for school, she never forgets to kiss me goodbye and say I love you, and she does the same whenever I leave the house.
- When I leave the house, Mckenzie says, "Wait Mummy! I love you and will miss you." When I turn around, I face this beautiful mirror framed with flowers and bright colours, showing me that I can get so caught up in life that I forget the little things that make people feel appreciated and loved.

The last quality mirrored, in my son Benjamin, is the most important quality of integrity and honesty. When you make a promise, keep it, or don't make it at all.

- Many times, as parents, we tend to brush our children's requests off by promising something else, or to do it another time. This happens to me if I am working on the computer and Benjamin comes to me to play a game. He loves board games. I would hardly pay attention, and would reply, "Yes, Benjamin, I will play with you tomorrow.
- Most times, if we break a promise, kids just eventually take it as a reality, feel hurt, and move on. Not my Benjamin—he calls me on it! He will say, "Mom, you promised!"

How can I be that person who asks people to trust me when *my word is not my word!* So now, I only make promises I can keep, and nothing will stop me from keeping the promises I make.

We always hope that our children do as we say and not what we do, *so look at what they mirror from you, and if it is a trait you do not like, change yourself before you try and change that behavior in them.* But they are more than that. They also do better than we do, and if we appreciate that our children can teach us as much as we teach them, then we too become better people. Just like I learnt how to:

- Accept people for who they are and not for who you want them to be.
- Value the power of kind words.
- Keep promises, or don't make them in the first place.

One of the things I did to put my mindset into this mirroring of my children, was that I looked at their peaceful faces when they were sleeping, and I looked into their beautiful mirrors, and I saw qualities I could learn from them, and could start to mirror them.

Chapter 6

THE SCENARIOS GAME

The Scenarios game is a game that my co-host and I have in our parent online course, Interpersonal Parenting. My co-host, Phil Edwards, was actually my instructor for Interpersonal Communications and Sociology. After I finished the course a month later, and my eight-year-long radio show in Jamaica was cancelled because I moved to Canada, I thought Phil would make a really good host for the show. He is a Canadian, born to Jamaican Canadian parents, and I am Jamaican born and live in Canada, so it made a good mix. I was practicing all the interpersonal communication skills, but Phil taught me the theory, so now I was able to explain my techniques to others. Then I took the Group Dynamics course with Louisa Iannaci, where I learnt the theory and group dynamics and conflict resolution. With the two courses, I thought we could teach these tools in a fun family way by creating games. Scenarios was the first of many games that Phil and I designed to help families with their communication, conflict resolution, mediation, and creating harmony in the home.

With our Caribbean roots, we want to make the online course affordable to everyone, so you have two options. The first option is to do the course by yourself, where we give you the video tutorials and all the templates so that you can guide your family to harmony. The second option is an eight-week coaching course, where you get the regular course, but Phil and I personally coach your family, and facilitate the games via online video calls. Of course, a free bonus in this book is a coupon code for a discount on the courses and our online parent's club membership.

Why did Phil and I choose games to teach such serious issues? How do these games reduce the arguments and stress, to create harmony in your home? Before I answer these questions, let me take the chance to give homage to my favourite parenting authors. First, the man that inspired me to be a parent coach, and helped me through the worst part of my life, is Kevin Leman. His books helped me start my journey into self-reflection and identity. The book, *Have a New You by Friday*, helped me to discover why I act the way I do, and how I react to situations. Again, I worked on myself so that I could then work on my children. Check out free bonuses for a special discount on my favourite parenting books.

So, back to work. Children, and even us, learn when it is fun. Also, we all learn differently. Some learn in a tactile way (by doing), and it is better that we learn by acting out the scenario than being in the heat of the moment. Some are audio learners (listening), some are verbal (they teach to learn), and some are visual (see it to believe it). There are also combinations, but I get into that more in another chapter. This game targets each type of learning to teach behaviors to have in family situations, and most importantly, in a fun way. It also teaches us parents to set the ground rules *before* playing, and not during or after. For example, for the sensitive in the family, the rules are as follows:

The facilitator teaches the strategies to manage emotions when the scenario gets confrontational:

- Use the emotion meter (in the game pieces, everyone gets one).
- Use the de-escalation techniques you have identified in the meter, like breathing. Say positive self-talk in your mind, taking a break from the game or a stress tool from your box (a list of items is in the game rules).

- Monitor nonverbal messages.
- The winner is the one who matches the best reactions to the scenarios, not accusing others of their worst in the past. It is a game and is hypothetical, not an opportunity to make personal attacks on your family members.

The key to this game is to laugh and not fight. Even by establishing the rules and goals of the game, you will be able to stop the arguing and create harmony. Many of my parents are shocked how the game works so well, and not only do they teach the kids to handle situations at home better, but they also learn themselves. Parenting is truly an exchange you will learn from your children as much as you teach them.

Also, you are placed in a neutral environment, and use active listening and learn about non-verbal messages. A family that learns together grows in strength. My father used to tell us all the time that the world is hard, and we need to stick together. He would tell us the story of how my mother's grandfather called his five boys together and asked them to bring two sticks. When they returned, their father told them to give him one stick each and keep one. Then he told them to break their stick, and they did that easily. He asked them if it was easy to break it, and they replied yes. He then put the sticks together and told each of them to try and break them. Each son could not. He then told them, "You see what happens when you are separate and do not work together. You will break easily, but when you stick together, you are each other's strength. Your individuality complements each other, and you will not break easily. Those brothers ended up running an empire of companies and assisting Jamaica to becoming independent. This story told me to teach major lessons once to all my children, and not three times. But hey, let's make it fun!

Scenarios is a game where we explain everyday life; however, we're not experiencing the same scenario in the moment and with negative emotions. Each round has a facilitator who has specific instructions to teach positive tools in mediation and to stop any emotional turn in the game. With each scenario, you have to ask your family if they are in the scenario.

- **Accommodator** – The family member that gives up all their wants to please the others. *I lose/you win.*
- **Competitor** – The family member that makes sure their wants are above the others. *I win/you lose.*
- **Avoider** – The family member that runs away from conflict, at the cost of their own wants. *I lose/you lose.*
- **Compromiser** – The family member that gives up more to the competitor but gives less than the accommodator. *I win and lose/you win and lose.*
- **Collaborator** – The problem solver. This family member works out a solution that works with everyone, so that nobody gives up anything, or everyone gives a little. *I win/you win.*

The facilitator (who changes in every turn) aims to get each member to learn the following, by asking the following questions of each player:

- In this scenario, identify your feelings, needs, and interests.
- If you were (point to *another player)* in this scenario, what would you do?
- What triggers you in this scenario?
- In this scenario, what do we need to do so everyone wins?

The facilitator is an important role in this game, as it teaches mediation and active listening skills. Active listening is being present when someone is speaking, by listening to their words, observing their body language, and hearing their tone of voice. This includes eye contact. Nod your head, respect their perspective, maintain an open stance, ask questions to clarify what the speaker is saying, and acknowledge when the other is speaking. Also, put your own thoughts aside and concentrate on the other person; be there mentally, not just physically; don't rush the speaker; look for cues that will help you see how the speaker is feeling; or interrupt and keep an open mind! (Mckinley & Ross, 2008)

One example of a scenario we play in the game is *How Do We Say It*. It gives scenarios that pose conflict, and when two players want something, they get it through how they speak. I use this example as it is personal to me.

You see, in my marriage, and later in my life, I was surrounded by aggressive, NOT Assertive, messaging, to which I was never assertive. People in my life constantly used aggressive messaging, and I would only respond with non-assertive messaging. I still do, and in most instances in my life, I am always walked over and taken advantage of. After five years of being apart (however, my sister is still in my life), I am still not achieving the four major behaviors that demonstrate assertive messaging, because I did not learn it.

- I am starting to but rarely express my feelings frankly and openly to people in general, including romantic relationships.
- I still avoid expressing my feelings, opinions, and beliefs in order to avoid conflict and stressful situations.
- I do not stand up for my rights in order to avoid conflicts.
- I accept what others say.

My children have encouraged my assertive messages because I am assertive for them. That too was not a good thing because I am not teaching them to be assertive. Assertive behavior enables you to act in your own interests without denying the rights of others. This is a behavior to teach our children. Assertive people are more open, less anxious, more contentious, and less likely to be intimidated or easily persuaded. Would you not love your children and yourself to be like that? Also, if we are assertive, we are harmonious. If we are aggressive, we are hostile. See where I am going here?

In the online course, the teacher that taught me is my co-writer for the online course. I am still learning to be more assertive. I have to admit that after taking the course, I realized the peace in my house was because I was teaching my children to be assertive, but I was still not being assertive myself. The exercise is in the online course that I did, and along with my thirty classmates, I found it insightful and an experience full of growth. When our parents did the Time to Shine, My Words Are Mine exercise, they loved it. Each family member enjoyed doing their presentation; it was their time to shine. The older siblings helped the younger ones, and they said, once they can talk, they can do it.

Back to Scenarios, we do explore the different behaviors and messaging. The game helps to identify, just like the Time to Shine, How We Speak, especially in a conflict. We recommend that the family do Time to Shine before Scenarios, so when our families play Scenarios, they can identify what is happening.

So, I mentioned my non-assertive messaging—what is it? It is opposite to aggressive. I like to say that assertive behavior is the balance between aggressive and non-assertive behavior, which are two extremes, and I definitely have the habit of going between the two extremes. You see, when I am non-assertive in conflict, it is *you win, I lose*. So when I am fed up with losing, I go the other way and be aggressive in conflict, where *you lose, I win!*

So, in the game, we present scenarios that actually are potential conflicts that can be in the family, and the key to the game is actually a team game where both players have to ensure that both win. There's actually a collaboration. How we use our words achieves this goal. If everyone wins, then we create harmony. If you are like I was, you would eventually feel fed up with losing and get angry to win, always causing conflict and fighting.

As a non-aggressor, I was an avoider and an accommodator; if I was lucky, I would be able to get a compromise. But it all was up to the other person and how they were feeling. Let me expand on this. So, I would avoid conflict at any cost, especially with my ex-husband; and you see, I always would maintain that our children learn relationships and interacting within a relationship from their parents. What happened was that I was in a marriage where I had an aggressor. I married an aggressor because that aggressor showed me love, whereas I had grown up with aggressors who did not show me love, or conditional love, I should say.

So, what I was teaching my children was to be a non-assertive person in order to handle an aggressor, because that's how I handled my relationship in my marriage. In order to avoid conflict, and in order to avoid more arguments, I just kept quiet. I avoided even bringing up things that I wanted or needed, even for the children, and what it taught my kids, especially in the male-female nuclear family image, was to be aggressors. That's why I developed the game, because I hoped that when we played the game as a family, we could see how we handle conflicts, and the facilitator would be able to know the right way and teach each person, even the husband and wife, or the mother and father, to be able to be an assertive person. You see, that's why I call it a family game; we have an environment where a wife can actually teach her husband how to be more assertive instead of more aggressive, or vice versa.

The aggressive role I'm messaging is all about winning. Now remember, I said earlier that I was a non-aggressive, but there were times when I became an aggressor because I got so fed up. In other words, it's one extreme to the other, and we can go one extreme to the other when we're ready, and when you deal with conflict in extremes, it creates stress and fighting.

Aggressors are more about competing, and they may compromise when they're in the mood or when they're less on the aggressive scale, meaning that it's all about them winning and you losing. Most times, when an aggressor is confronted by assertiveness, you will get the compromising. However, remember that we're aiming for collaboration, which is the highest level, where you have concern for the other person, and concern for yourself, and everybody wins. When two assertive people get together, and they deal with the conflict, or they deal with a scenario in the game, your goal is to find a way where everybody wins. The facilitator's main role is to paraphrase what everyone is saying in order to handle the scenario, and once everybody feels good that they have left that scenario as a winner, then they have collaborated and, therefore, won a point.

Now, as I said before, I was an aggressor at times because I got so fed up with mostly being an unknown aggressor. However, when someone is an aggressor on a continuous basis, we have to look at deeper things with that personality type. The key is to help an aggressor, who usually has a strong personality, to see that assertiveness and aggression are completely two different things. So many parents that have taken the online course, Interpersonal Parenting, have seen a difference in their spouses who are normally aggressive, because this lesson is taught in such a subtle way that they don't even realize that they're switching their mode of communication, and they don't take offense because they're not being accused of being an aggressor. In the game, you should never point out that somebody is an aggressor. Stick to the scenarios, let the facilitator do their job, and the outcomes will be different—I promise. Remember to go to my website for bonuses for this online course.

When dealing with a child that has already developed an aggressor behavior (Notice that I say *aggressor* behavior, not *aggressive*. I've purposely done that because one thing I learnt from reading and studying—and it is effective—is that you never punish the child or discipline the child, because sometimes it is the action of the child that needs punishment, so we're talking about the behavior, not the child, because the behavior can change.), the same scenario happens, but you can actually highlight it and say, "Hey, how can we handle this scenario differently; how can everyone win?" Because right now, you're winning and they're losing. It's going to take some time to change behaviors; however, reinforcing the game, even after it's played and during the rest of the week, is a key thing. In other words, we give you the tools in the online course to reinforce the messages and have those teachable moments. A lot of times, we miss out on teachable moments because we don't have the script, and we don't know what to say.

So, I really hope you enjoy the game, Scenarios. You can go in the online course to get tidbits and samples with the free bonuses that I've given you. I've given you some templates and, in the book, I give you the theory behind the course. I hope it helps your family the way it helped my family and so many others.

Chapter 7

GO BACK THREE SPACES

So, I have one teenager, one leaving teenagehood and now a young man, and one entering teenagehood. During my radio show, in my workshops, and when doing public speaking at PTAs, churches, and parent functions, I had many parents come up to me and say that they cannot handle their teenager, and that they are out of control. Well, there's no good way to say this, but it's time for tweaking. I go back to what I said about my daughter: She had so many self- imaging techniques and strategies at 15, because I made the mistake of thinking that I could take her off the spectrum.

My twenty-year-old, has a tendency to not be as considerate as he should be. He's a bit selfish (he's going to kill me for writing this in the book), and tweaking him is a little harder because I am now full in consultancy stage. Hopefully, what I say to him gets through. I say things to him in a constructive way. I don't say things like, "Hey, you know this is not working," and most times, with him, I wait till he comes to me. I'm really blessed that way because I've always been non-judgmental with them, and I've always had the techniques that I've used over the years, which have benefited me because they feel comfortable to come to me with anything, and to ask my advice as a consultant. My 12-year-old, who is going through puberty, has things that I need to change. Again, he's been through divorce. So have my daughter and my oldest son. They've been through life challenges that their father and I have created. Why are we not surprised that our children are reacting negatively to them? Then we turn around and we have to punish them again. It goes back to self-reflection, communication, figuring out how to relate to them, and taking ownership of our part to play when it comes to this tweaking process.

That's why it was actually easy to name this chapter, Go Back Three Spaces. At the teenage stage, that's exactly what we're doing. We have to go back, reassess the situation, and see how we can handle the behavior differently, because you definitely have to handle it differently. They're older now, and you can't just use the star chart, and you can't use timeouts. You have to know and be able to negotiate and reason with them, and apologize, apologize, apologize. Say sorry, and mean it. By changing your actions, after saying sorry, it makes a huge impact in your child's life. And what do they do? They learn to do it themselves.

I always say that this is your last chance to do any tweaking because, as I said, with my eldest, I'm now a consultant. I can't wake him now; I have to hope that he sees or identifies problems that he has in his life, and comes to me and asks me for advice, but all I can do is give him advice. He has the choice to take it or not, as a last chance to deal with making any behavioral changes. From tween to teen, but more importantly in the tween stage, look at the bad behaviors and whether you need to say, "Hold on, where did I go wrong with this child, and how do I improve it?" Apologize, and make the change, and tell them that you're changing your parenting style because their behavior is obviously a result of what you did wrong. Tell them what you did wrong, and say that you're sorry, and that you're going to improve on it because you want them to be the best person they can be in life.

This goes back to saying that bad behavior equals bad parenting. You may be the most giving parents in the world, but through the divorce, you never had a lot of time with your children, or you worked really hard and you gave lots of presents, and you gave them the life you never had. Well, one child may appreciate all the things that you've worked hard for and have given them, but the second child might have said, "Hold on, I want your time. I don't want you working so hard, and I'm going to make sure that I get your time." This brings me to a saying I always use: Good attention and bad attention are the same things to a child if that is the only attention they know. This is also extended as *sick attention.* Let me explain. If you only have time for your children when they are misbehaving, or if you only give them your attention to punish them, that attention is the same attention that you use to reward them or spend time with them. Even worse, if you only give them attention when they get sick (because you're like, okay, I have to stop work because my child is sick), they will get sick to get your attention.

So, encourage yourself to ensure that you give them the positive attention, meaning that you don't abuse it. And you don't say that you're not going to give them attention if they behave badly, because that's actually abuse. Favoritism is also abuse. Yes, when you very blatantly favor one child over the other because that child behaves the way you want them to, you're punishing the child with your emotion, and that is called emotional abuse. If you don't pay attention to them because they don't act the way you want them to act, then that, my friends, is emotional abuse. What I'm referring to is rewarding them and structuring your attention, so that they can count on your attention on these days.

If you are a busy entrepreneur, and you work really hard to provide for your children, that's great. I'm not knocking you; trust me on that one, because I work just as hard, as I am a mother. What I do though is to schedule time with them, and they know that it's happening. I schedule time as a family, so Sunday is adventure day. We take turns picking an adventure, and each person gets to pick one every Sunday when it's their turn. I also schedule at least one hour a week with each child, and here's the key: They pick the activity, not you. You have to do what they want you to do, and even if it is just taking them to where they want to go and dropping them off, make sure you're there and that they can count on you for that one hour a week. That way you don't have to rely on good attention and bad attention. Rewarding your children with emotion, or punishing your children by withholding emotion, is a slippery slope.

Then we throw the hormones into the game. Oh, my goodness, I'm going to bring up yet another book because, as a single mother of boys, I needed this book, and it made a lot of sense. So here is my little gift to you, A book that is great to read if you have boys is by Steve Biddulph. called "Raising Boys".. It is highly recommended and explains how boys go through puberty, and how we as women can cause them to be so irritated just by the tone or the level of our voice when they're in puberty. You can get the link to buy the book, on my website listed above.

However, on the flip side, don't let these puberty hormones actually be an excuse to let them off the hook. Be aware of them, be aware of your communication styles, and be aware that you might have to deescalate faster in a conflict than you would normally, but you still have to be able to communicate and get what you need out of them. This is a time to be the most understanding and to dig deep for patience. Knowing I got through the terrible two's and three's it helped me, and it's apparent that I've worked to be the most vulnerable for your children, and when I say vulnerable, I mean showing more empathy. And yes, our children never think that we were their age; however, it's because we actually don't tell them or relate to them on their level. We just say, "Oh, I was your age once, and I handled it. Why can't you?" No, we did not; we were just as emotional, because we were children.

If you truly dig deep within yourself, you'll see that you can be vulnerable with them. Say, "Hey, when I was your age, nobody liked me in school. My personality was so much like yours, but it gets better." And I even let them know how their grandfather (my father) would help me through it, and how their uncle (my brother) said to me, when I couldn't understand people my age, "Hang with my friends," and he would take me everywhere with his friends, and I was able to be included in a group. I loved it, and all his friends took care of me. Tell your children the stories. Tell them about yourself when you were growing up—the good, the bad, and the ugly—and let them realize you are a real person, and that you went through real issues; you got through it and you got married, or you had them and you're happy.

Remember, if you're not happy, you need to make yourself happy somehow, because they sense it, they see it, and they know it. And if you are not happy, the first person they blame is themselves. Tweak their bad behavior, tweak their outbursts, and tweak their depression. Finding out who they are at that time is also a way to tweak yourself. Even if you technically had your children in your twenties, and whether you're now in your early twenties, your early thirties, your early forties, or in your midlife, right now is where you're starting to reflect on yourself, and by bringing them into your reflection, you can bring them into your process.

I actually made that mistake. I was going through a whole new process when I was in my forties. I had recently divorced and had been through trauma myself, and was discovering who I really am. I was discovering who I have been all my life, and I started tweaking myself at 40. They saw that, and I brought them into the process of my tweaking. My teenagers were able to evolve with me, but they didn't think it was funny because I wasn't doing it to them; I was doing it as a family, and I dubbed it the Tweaking game. Again, this game is in the online course, and it is a lot of fun. I give you a few tips at the end of the book, as a prize.

And now we reach the age of the sexes game, and I don't mean that we're going to actually have a sex game—this is about talking about sex. We get that letter sent home from school, telling us that they are going to talk to them about the sexual reproduction system, and all about sex, in health class. Personally, I appreciate that they actually bring up the subject. They talk about all the different types of feelings you may have. I'm glad that they don't just bring up heterosexuality, but they also bring up homosexuality. Now, in the world that we live in, our children are knowing way more than we did at their age. In fact, my twelve-year-old comes home and teaches me about transgender, and how not to genderize him, and he is quite entertaining with it. I appreciate the talk, and I don't shut them down.

My children are completely comfortable talking to me about sex, because I have been completely comfortable talking to them about it. I have to thank my parents for that; they were very open with their affection, but they were very classy about it. They didn't do anything in front of us, but we knew, when the door was locked, not to even knock. They also spoke about what was decent in public and what wasn't decent in public. But the biggest thing that they did for us was that they left the communication door open on the subject. We could ask our parents anything we wanted about sex, because that door was open. We were never curious about sex; therefore, whenever our friends were telling us the wrong information, we could tell them that it doesn't sound right, and we would be able to go home and clarify it. And you know, we weren't so obsessed about sex. We even knew that you don't have sex just because you're lacking attention or affection, and that you don't do it out of curiosity or for popularity.

I talk more about this in my workshops and my online course, and I do a whole chapter and a segment on teaching; but I mainly use that when parents ask me how to deal with it, if they have that problem. And because we do have to take into consideration cultural influences and religious influences, we can't go about doing it; the only people that can teach our children about sex are their parents, because other people shouldn't be doing it for them. But it has to be taught, and it is so important.

When I was younger, in my Performing Arts Company, we had a big issue on teen pregnancy and sexual transmitted disease. When I was a teenager, AIDS was coming to the forefront, and a lot of research was being done. We were hired by an international organization to write a show on it, to teach teenagers about sex and sexually transmitted diseases, and how it is dealt with. The research helped us because we actually had a lot of scenes in the play on parenting, and we showed two different types of situations. One was where a girl and I actually helped write the part, and it was my role, where my parents spoke about sex with me, and I had a stance of abstinence. The second situation was about my best friend. Nobody spoke to her about sex, and she didn't know anything about sex, and then we had other influencers.

So, it was a really good show, and the main thing we did was to encourage teenagers at the show. We taught them about sexually transmitted diseases, and what would happen if you got pregnant, and things like that, but we especially encouraged teenagers to go home and talk to their parents about it, and we sent pamphlets home. We did not talk to them about sex for their parents; we just gave them the facts, but in regard to the emotional side, we encouraged the parents to talk to them about it. So, I touch on it in this book, because it is communication. How do you communicate?

How do you talk about a subject you really don't want to talk about? How do you talk to your children about masturbation and age appropriateness? Studies show that from age two, boys will start wondering what that thing is between their legs and all we say to them is, don't touch!" so they grow up feeling embarrassed that they want to touch it unless we speak to them. I mean, I freaked out when I opened a diaper and saw it sticking up. So, when the opportunity came up to talk about touching yourself or sex, I always had this stance where I would I speak about it. I took the opportunity to speak about it, and I would tell them in age appropriate ways (you know, like where babies come from, and how Mommy and Daddy are pieces of a puzzle, and how the pieces come together), and then as they grew older, I spoke about it a little bit more.

When they came home from that class, they would ask me questions, and as much as I would cringe to answer the questions, I knew I had to do it because it helped me. And they knew they could come to me because I left the door so wide open that before they have sex with anyone, they could come to me and ask me the questions first. As my children got older, I told them that you personally have sex when you can afford the consequences; meaning, if you have a job and can afford it, maybe that's when you should take the risk of having a child, because that's what sex is. I did not tell them that sex was bad. Sex is lovely; we all love it, and it feels good. However, I did tell them about the consequences.

So, let me sum up the sex game: Use appropriate language (sometimes use code words, like slugging, or that thing, or private parts). Talk about masturbation and appropriate places to do it, and whether it is appropriate or not to do it, depending on your cultural and religious beliefs. But the key to this game is that you leave the sex door wide open, so that they can always come and talk to you.

At this time in their lives, they are going through so many challenges. I thank God every day that I don't have to go through being a teenager again. When you're not an adult yet, you're given responsibilities. Some teenagers, at this point, are age 15, and some of them are even aged 18, and yet due to autism or other exceptionalities, they have the mindset and social adaptability of someone five years younger than they are. So, they're misjudged, and it's a really hard life as they get older, especially if they have exceptionalities. So, how do we give our children the tools for these challenges? How do we communicate with them? Again, you play that open door policy, where they can come to you at any time. This is a key to this age: When they have a problem, they know they can go to Mom and Dad, and they will be their biggest sounding board.

However, if you cannot be there because you may have clashing personalities, make sure that they find that caring adult that they can talk to. The biggest thing not to do is to be judgmental in everything, and it's hard, because your emotions are there; this is your child, and you don't want to listen. They're hurting, and you want to solve the problem, or sometimes you don't want to see them hurting, so you'd want to hear the problem.

So, it is a tricky age, but one thing that has helped me is noting who they are, identifying their strengths, and ensuring that when they come with the challenge, we look at their strengths and how to handle the challenge using their strength, and all we end up doing in this game is providing them with the confidence to handle the challenge. A lot of times, they don't have the confidence to handle the challenge, and that's when issues happen. Or when the challenge is bigger, and they're reacting to you and taking it out on you, I wonder where they learnt that. They could be taking it out on you when they're upset, just as we did it to them when they were growing up—so again, tweak those behaviors, saying that you know.

I know the times when I've been angry or had a bad day at work, or I've had challenges trying to run the house, and I show them that I have been angry with them. "I am really sorry. I'm going to try and do better, but can you be aware that you are doing that to me?" Work through the challenge instead of being that separate stick. Remember that tweaked analogy: Instead of us working apart, let's work together and beat that challenge together.

This comes to the biggest weakness of all in our behavior: We have not been playing with our children. So, you've read this book, your children are teenagers, and you're like, "Oh, my gosh, what am I going to do? My child is out of control. I have not been spending time because I've been working hard." I'm not judging you, so please don't think that I am, because everybody's life is different. People are single parents, they're working hard, and they need to put food on the table.

Nobody's judging you, and there's no such thing as a bad parent once you're willing to make some sort of effort and not abuse your children. I may complain about my mother and her parenting styles but I cannot never say she did not love me or care about me. And you know what? Kudos to you. Great job for even picking up this book and reading it, because it means you want to be a great parent to your child, and that is what you're doing when you pick up a book or you buy a book on parenting. You are saying, "Hey, I want to be the best I can be," and no parent is the same; just as no child is the same.

So, congratulations! This may be your first book that you started reading, or it may be your second, third, or fourth book, but you're making the change that you need. What I'm really saying in this chapter is to go back 3 spaces; tweak yourself as a human being; make sure you make yourself happy so that your kids will be happy; and make sure that you say sorry to your children for the mistakes you make, or for those that you have made in the past in your parenting or as an adult. Apologize and change your behavior. I always tell my children, when they say sorry to me, to not say sorry unless they're going to not do it again, or they're going to change their behavior. Other than that, don't bother saying sorry. So that's another thing, parents. Don't say sorry if you're not going to change a behavior. When you mindfully say that you're sorry for not spending enough time with your children, it is really saying that you're also going to spend more time with them. This is our chance to go back 3 spaces and tweak ourselves, as we tweak our kids. Good luck.

Chapter 8

WHEN THE GAME CHANGES

Well, I have definitely had my game change. I have three children with dyslexia, and one child with autism, and we're still looking into auditory processing disorder for my eldest. I would say that the biggest tool you need when your game changes in a family is recognizing your instincts. You know your child when it comes to something being wrong, and doctors do not know your child the way you do. If you have a nagging feeling that something's wrong with your child, whether it be learning exceptionality, emotional exceptionality, mental exceptionality, or physical, don't rest till you find all the help they need to succeed in life. Physical exceptionalities are easy to identify; the others are much harder.

The first exceptionality was dyslexia. My eldest son was actually misdiagnosed and was told that he's just a tactile learner. At this time, I was living in Jamaica, and they have one type of school system, and this is where I coined the term, *learning exceptionalities*, and that our teachers have *teaching disabilities*. He was also an amazing athlete. So, unfortunately, the teachers did not know how to handle him, and he kept failing his exams no matter how hard he studied. It was not until he reached high school that it really started showing its ugly head.

I listened to the initial diagnosis and didn't trust my instincts when he failed exams. I would say that he didn't study enough, even though I personally would study with him when he was suffering in school.

The coaches would call me and say that they needed him to play, and to make sure he played, and he couldn't go to extra lessons because I thought I was at least letting him do what he's good at to get his confidence up. However, when he started feeling that we were punishing him and stopping him from doing sports so that he could get his grades up, I eventually got fed up, and I said that something is wrong, and I took him to get reassessed. Sure enough, he had dyslexia. We diagnosed him at 13, but not much could be done by then. In fact, right now, at 19, I'm taking him to get auditory processing disorder testing, because now they're saying it might not be dyslexia, and it might be this.

But he is a success story because when I discovered that he did have dyslexia, I heard about these glasses that come in the right color to suit them. It helps them to read, and it diffuses their reading, helping them to read faster and better and more accurately. The doctor who discovered these dyslexia glasses lived in England. I would not give up. I phoned every ophthalmologist in Jamaica to find out if they knew anything about it, and if they didn't know anything about it, I asked if they could learn it. I found a lovely young Jamaican doctor who studied in England with the man who invented the glasses. I called her, but she didn't have the material because she didn't think any of that was happening in Jamaica. So, she improvised and got the starting material and tested my son. Sure enough, if you have a nagging feeling that something's wrong with your child, whether it be a learning exception on the emotional, mental, or physical exceptionality, don't trust that you will find all the help they need to succeed in life. Physical exceptionality is easier to identify; the others are much harder.

The biggest tip I'm giving in this chapter, and starting with this chapter, is to never give up on helping your children to overcome exceptionalities. It may force our children to work harder, but that doesn't mean it cannot be achieved. Try and spend the money to find out what can be done to help them to succeed, no matter what exceptionality they have. I say to them all the time that an exceptionality is not a disability, and it does not make life impossible or the task impossible; it just makes it harder.

Our key as a parent with a child with an exceptionality is to show that we advocate for them at all times, and not just advocate for them, but to also teach them to advocate for themselves as well. With my daughter and my youngest son, I taught them how to advocate for themselves and not to feel embarrassed to ask for extra time for exams, or when they need help, or need to sit in the front in order to hear. I give them all the tools that they need to succeed. That's where I spend the money—not on gifts. If they need iPads to take to school to do the notes and to take verbal notes and record notes, then they will get the iPad for school.

This type of family definitely has to communicate differently, and we have to communicate at different levels. I feel very blessed to have children with exceptionalities because I think that has given me a different way to look at how I communicate, especially with a child with autism, where communication and social skills are constantly in the teaching mode. When you have children that learn differently, you have children that communicate differently. One of the things I've actually learned how to do is communicate like an engineer, and I made a profession of it because I used to say that I gave birth to an engineer. So, I know how to speak to them, and they have such a technical mind and a logical mind that I have learned how to almost translate into layman's terms. Being artistic myself, I've learned how to also communicate at that level.

They're so smart that I've had to learn how to communicate at that level as well, especially since I have children that think so differently than I do. I was forced to learn how they think in order to communicate better, and the results, I found, were not just that I could get through to them, but also that the house was becoming less hostile and more harmonious. I found that if we were stubborn and stuck to our ways as parents, we would just end up fighting with our kids because they're at a level where they're learning and want to be accepted, and they will have challenges, and we should take that into consideration when having children with exceptionalities. I do not want to offend, but my life is so special because my daughter with autism was the greatest gift that I have received, and she has made me not only a better parent but also a better person. I know that not all parents with children with exceptionalities feel that way, and I'm fortunate that my daughter is a level one, and she communicates to assert, and she can speak very well. Her nonverbal skills are non-existent, but I'm very blessed that she has the level one autism.

It does not mean I'm belittling or degrading parents who get frustrated easily, because I have gotten frustrated easily, and I have been tired. In fact, in my day profession, I have chosen to not work with children with autism, or to work with the parents, because I want to be able to go home to my daughter and be fresh to deal with her and communicate with her. I feel that if I had to work with children all day, I would be too tired to come home and handle my daughter.

The other thing I learned about children, by having a child with autism, is that every child is different. Yes, they may be labeled with autism or labeled with dyslexia, but again, I have three children with dyslexia, and all three children have a different type of dyslexia. My daughter has dyslexia where she can't see the middle of the words, so no matter how hard she tries, she can't spell. My two sons can read, and they can spell; they just can't understand what they're reading because it's all over the place. Their comprehension is low, so learning how to communicate differently is a key, and learning how to play the game differently is also a key. In my online course, I do have a section for autism, as well as games that I have learned how to play when it comes to the emotional self-regulation model, and it didn't just work with my daughter; it has worked with all three of kids.

I think the biggest challenge I've had is with the siblings. They all have their own exceptionalities, my daughter having the worst one in the sense of dealing with it, and the dependency that she has on me has created some jealousy in the household. Both my boys feel that I have given her way too much attention, and that I am a helicopter parent and she revels in it. This is unfair because no matter how hard I try to explain to them what autism is (I guess because I'm still learning, because it's still evolving), they don't tend to understand. Most families' siblings are very tolerant when it comes to their siblings having exceptionalities, but apparently there are a few cases where siblings get jealous, or they just don't have anything to do with them. I don't know where I went wrong; I'm still trying to figure that out. In a way, I have. As I said earlier in the chapter, I treated her like I had taken her off the spectrum, but now we all had to accept that she's not. I have accepted it, but my boys haven't. I'm working on them, and she isn't trying to change a dialogue with that.

However, life has always given me circumstances to help me teach my children (when they are with certain family members), especially my youngest son, who didn't accept my daughter but ended up having to defend her. Other outside family members would turn to my daughter and say that she doesn't have autism. Because of those ignorant family members, I've been able to see a change in my youngest son when he saw it from another side and how it affected her; and therefore, I'm very grateful to those ignorant family members for helping me turn my son into a more compassionate child when it comes to exceptionalities.

This brings me to the saying: How do you play a game when not everyone wants to play it? How do you reopen your extended family members? How do you teach them when they don't want to believe it, because it's just a different way of thinking? How do you protect your children from that ignorance? Again, it's all down to communication, and sometimes you have to deal with not being invited to family functions. Sometimes you have to deal with the constant comments that you're a bad mother, which I did receive when my daughter was younger and she was having the temper tantrums, but I had to grow a thick skin. Again, do whatever it takes to help your child to succeed—do the research.

There's so much on the internet. Find clubs, find associations, or find a peer group that can support you so that you can help your child to succeed. And those family members who don't want to play the game, you can either tell them to step aside for the game or you can help them to join your family game and be included. If they don't want to play by your rules even after you have done everything you can to include them. Let it go; your job here is for your child, and that way you can teach him to say that not everybody wants to play the game, and not everybody's as tolerable, and people think differently. Just as we ask everyone to respect how different our children are, we also teach our children to respect how other people are different, and that not everybody is accepting. I guess we teach them to accept themselves so that they don't need acceptance from others.

This brings me to how important your team is when you have a child with an exceptionality. Sometimes a non-accepting player may even be your spouse. Many times, statistics show that fathers don't accept autism, so you even have to deal with that obstacle, and if you do, and you end up being a single parent of children with exceptionalities, get that team together. Don't be shy to find your support; don't be shy to find the doctors; don't be shy to find your associations, clubs, peers, and parents that can support you.

The fact that you're reading this book means that I'm part of your team, Phil is part of your team, and we're here to support you even in the words that you read right now. You're an amazing parent because you are parenting a child with an exceptionality. I'll always remember, no matter how hard it gets, that I am an exceptional mother because I parent and exceptional child. So, pat yourself on the back, pour a glass of wine, have a hot bath, pour some juice, and celebrate every achievement you have each day. Keep a journal of all your winnings that you had that day with your child, and say thank you and enjoy your wins, because you deserve it.

Here are a few things that you can do with team building. Again, find the family members that support you, and build your team from that support. If you cannot bring family members in on your team, and if they're not willing to participate, do not waste your time. They will come around, and if they don't come around, you will find others to replace them, because the time you spend trying to convince them to come around, you're taking away from your child who truly needs you. Remember your clubs, your associations, your doctors, your psychologist, and even your dentist, ophthalmologist, and ear and nose doctor. They have the new technology to find out all the things and all the information you need to help your children to succeed, and that's about all you want. You build your team with people that will help your child succeed, no matter what type of exceptionality they have.

Special Olympics is an amazing organization for children with exceptionalities, physically and mentally. The biggest thing that I did for my children was to find things they are good at, because confidence-building is the biggest gift you can give your child with an exceptionality. Once they have the confidence that they can achieve one thing, they will go out and achieve other things. My children have achieved many things. My son is aiming to be an engineer right now— the same one that had learning disabilities and was failing courses—and he's becoming a mechanic at the same time. He has not allowed his disabilities to hold him back, and that's because I gave him the opportunities to build his confidence, and the opportunities to find his talent. He is an extremely talented mechanic, and he loves cars. I asked my mechanic if he could apprentice for the summer, and sure enough, he loved it. He's gifted in it, and he's now pursuing that, as well as a university degree.

Your team can come from the most unusual places, so keep an eye out for those who can support you. Just know at all times, you will be fine and enjoy the wins even though a loss might come right after.

Chapter 9

HOW TO BE A GOOD COACH

So, let's find out how we can find opportunities for children to succeed, and how to give them the confidence they need in all aspects of their lives by balancing exploration and self-discipline. Why I say it like that is because when my children were discovering what type of activities they wanted to do, and how much time they had, it meant that they chopped and changed a lot. When they were younger in this discovery mode of activities, I would change their activities every term (semester), it went from dancing, table tennis, golf, sailing, athletics, art, music—I explained that if I saw some type of talent, I pushed them into that, and they would have to stick to it for each semester. As they got older it went from a term to a year. My eldest, as I mentioned several times, is an amazing athlete. One night, I had the pleasure of meeting Sir Sebastian Cole, who was the an Olympic champion, chairman of the London Organising Committee for the Olympic Games and a vice-president of the International Association of Athletics Federations (IAAF). At the time, my son was 10 years old, and I said to him, "Oh, my son is an amazing athlete, but he is not disciplined. How can I push him? What advice can you give me?" He told me that he did not start running till he was 11, and that was when he discovered what sports he liked to do. He said that when you push your children in competitive sports at too early of an age, they will drop out, because when he started running, all the other kids that were in it for longer, at his age, started dropping out, and he was just starting.

So, before the age of 11/12, let them have fun in their sports. Let them have fun in their activities to explore what they're good at and what they love to do. The time I use for exploration is summer. Summer is a time of discovery and a time for fun. Every summer, they discover their talents, and we cultivate their talents for the school year. So my daughter goes to baking camp, my son goes to chess and table tennis, and they go to golf or whatever they want to do. Now that they're at the age of sort of settling down in the talents that they've received, they now have to stick to it, and that's where the self-discipline comes in. Once they choose activities in September, they cannot give it up until summer exploration time. Don't encourage quitting activities right after they say that they don't like them, or they're tired of doing them. That's where you end up raising quitters, so once they've committed to a team, they must never let them down no matter what, and they must make the sacrifices for that team and that commitment until the actual activity is over.

The next thing I learnt with my three kids was the difference between cerebral talents versus tactile talents. Now, with my first two children, they definitely had tactile talents. My daughter is an artist, and she loves to bake and she loves to act. You could definitely find her talent very quickly. My oldest son is a natural athlete and is good at art. Again, very easy to identify. My youngest, however, is very good at chess. He is not the best, but he is very good. He played in national tournaments. He started late with chess, but he did very well in a short space of time. It was the same thing with table tennis; he did very well in a short space of time, and moved up in his division and age group very quickly. However, he didn't feel fulfilled, and even at 12 years old is like Mommy. I haven't found what I'm good at. I haven't found my purpose, and the fact that my twelve-year-old could actually say that and I still didn't clue in that the only reason he was saying that was because I was exposing him to only tactile opportunities and all he was feeling was he was not as good as his brother and sister.

What I realized with him is that he had what I called cerebral talents. He's a born leader, he loves sociology, he loves observing people, and like I said, just like me, he has interpersonal intelligence, and he can read people and speak to people very well. He actually makes quite a good comedian, so this summer I put him in leadership camp, and he loved it. I see this because I again made that mistake of not identifying it sooner, putting him into the traditional activities like sports and the arts, not realizing that there are other types of activities. And I should have known with the chess, because chess is a very suitable activity. However, where he found his true love and acceptance was Boy Scouts. The teamwork, the commandry, the skills learnt were all in his talent field. Also, having been raised by a single mother in a house of only women (my eldest now lives on his own) he enjoys having male role models and boys around him. Again, I looked at who I needed in my village, and Girl Guides and Boy Scouts was a must.

Sometimes your child chooses an activity that you have no clue about. Again, I enjoyed watching my son play chess; however, I did not know the game, and in a way I refused to know it, because then I'd look at the mistakes and freak out. So, when he was in tournaments, I just enjoyed watching their expressions. My eldest chose video games, and at first I was absolutely against it, but then it hit me. I'm against it because I don't understand it, and so I again researched it and realized that it is actually a profession. Many kids make money off of it. There are now the world games of Xbox, and it takes quite a bit of strategy. I would sit down and listen to him; my son who was previously a shy, quiet kid, became a leader and strategist when those head phones went on. So don't belittle these games. It is a new era and a new time, and if you take the time to learn these new activities before you judge them, your kids will be better off, because once they get your support, it's full speed ahead for them.

I did a workshop with at-risk youth. These were young men who were on probation for theft, drugs, and petty crimes. I worked with their parents, and I developed a rehabilitation program, which actually got 95% rehabilitation results with them. The program was called the Five Pillars of Personality, which most of these activities and these camps should be teaching, so when you're looking for these activities and camps, look for how they teach these five pillars of personality: 1.Self-discipline, 2. Self-respect, 3. Confidence, 4. Communication, and 5. Teamwork. Here are some ways I empowered the parents in this program.

The boys loved coming to the program, and I also used pet therapy because I ran the zoo in Jamaica, and I actually had the program at the zoo. I want to thank all the team players because it wasn't me; it was every member of the zoo team that worked on this program, and motivated these young men and made them part of a family, and they were amazing, so thank you. The parents had to sign their permission slip every day for them to come to the zoo to do the program, and how this empowered the parents is that they no longer had to beat their sons or show their sons that they have something very powerful to hold them accountable. In the contract at the beginning of the workshop, we wrote a contract for each young man to sign, and they knew what their responsibilities were, both at the camp and at home, and they knew what our responsibilities were to them, and that made a huge difference to the boys.

They had never had anybody tell them what they were responsible for. They never had adults to be accountable for them and to deliver things for them, and the partnership worked beautifully. The parents thanked us for the program because they no longer had to sign. Each person had an individual personality plan, and we sent it to them, and the parents had to check off yes if they did their homework, yes if they were polite to us tonight, and yes if they did their chores. The parents signed it and sent it to us, and they got bonuses at the camp, so camps can actually empower parents that need that help to be that judge and jury. The next day when they come here, they sign it, we praise them, and they earn points for their team in the camp because they did well at home the night before. This is something that can be done at home. Again, it's part of a workshop that I do, and I can do it with a group of kids, but I always go through the parents, because I'm not going to parent the children for them. I'm all about empowering the parents. When it comes to camps trying to parent their children, they actually undermine the parents.

Chapter 10

THE P.O.S.I.T.I.V.E. PARENTING PRIZE

I can truly sum up my parenting with one word: POSITIVE. I practice a P.O.S.I.T.I.V.E. approach to parenting:

Positiveness – My son calls me the hippie mom because I am always positive in thoughts and words.

Openness – I am open with them to the point of age appropriateness.

Supportive – I support their goals in life.

Interest – I take an interest in their lives, desires, and their goals. I communicate that, and their interests are important to me.

Truthfulness – Lying is the only thing that is punished in my home. They can make mistakes but must always own up to them. They are not punished for the mistake, no matter how bad it is, but they are punished for lying about it if they do.

Involvement – I am there when they need me and try to be there when they want me.

Value – I value my children as much as they value me.

Equality – My saying is: "The best gifts I can give my children are the opportunities to succeed and the support to do it." Equality is when I allow them to participate in decision making, and I even share the power when appropriate.

With everything that I've been through, especially after the separation and divorce, positivity has been my strongest tool, and no matter how many bad things you can experience in life, you can always find that silver lining and that positive aspect. However, do not fall into the trap that the positivity only hides the negative. You truly need to recognize and release the negative to be truly positive. Teaching myself to practice what I preach has helped me tremendously. I know that my kids sometimes get a little frustrated when I am too positive, but I can't help it. It keeps a smile on my face, and when they experience really big challenges or hard times, they come to me, and they appreciate me finding that silver lining for them. Sometimes they can't find it for themselves, so positivity has been the greatest tool, and with positivity comes thankfulness. Thankfulness is waking up every morning and being thankful for whatever you have, and it really starts your day right. I keep a journal of thankfulness, and I write in it every morning and every evening. I'm writing how thankful I am for my children every day, which helps me to appreciate them first thing in the morning and at the end of every day. This creates harmony in my home.

In my previous chapters, I also say how open I am with my kids. I talk about anything and everything with them. Sometimes I have quite a few TMI moments with my kids, and I cringe inside, but I do appreciate how open I am with them, and that they are open with me. Being open also means not being judgmental, and sometimes being judgmental means you want to discipline them for their actions, so you have to be careful, or at least I have to be careful about being judgmental or wanting to fix things or find solutions. But being open for them to talk to me and help them find their own solutions has been the key to the openness that I have with my kids.

You can always see that the openness is age-appropriate. Your rules change at each stage of their lives, which also helps with your openness and adjusting to when you get to that consultant stage. That is the hardest age, especially with my boys. I felt like I was looking for a window, and they would open the window and phone to talk to me, but only when they wanted to. This is hard for me because I was an active mom, but I have to appreciate the role I had, and love the new rules, and once that happens again, hopefully the window will actually open even wider, and stay open.

I'm my children's biggest cheerleader. I give them the opportunities every day. That's where I spend my money, by paying for the opportunities for them to succeed. I will budget their dreams, their aspirations, and their talents with anything that I have. However, I have to admit that buying presents has become difficult now because they're not into material things. I ask them what they want for their birthdays, and they say they don't know or they want tools for their opportunities like, baking supplies, magic the gathering cards, table tennis things etc. I actually buy their birthday experience I don't buy presents for them and you know it gives them great memories, happy memories they retell and the biggest success measure I have for their parties if they have fun not the guests.. Because I supported my children's dreams, my daughter has achieved things at her age in baking and culinary arts, and if I had not supported it, she would have been just dreaming about it. The biggest thing I've taught my children though is to not just talk about it but to do it, because Mommy is there to ensure that you take action, and even if you fail, you have learnt, you move on, and you try something else until you find what you're really good at. At a very early age, I had never been able to find out what they were good at, but I supported their opportunities to discover their talents.

But I don't just pay for the opportunity and send them on their way; I actually take interest in what they do. In my parent coaching, people ask me how they can connect with their child, and they will give me some areas where they connect with one child, but they don't connect with the other, and they don't know how to do it. They try and guess when I ask what they are doing with that child that they aren't connecting with. 90% of the parents that I speak to say that they do the regular things. They go to the museums or go to the beaches. They do activities that are family oriented, but the kids aren't interested. I smile and I say, "Well, have you asked them what they want to do, because I'm hearing that they are doing what you want them to do, or what you think they want to do.

I will give you my example. My son plays Magic the Gathering now, and I could say to him, "Okay, let's go for lunch, or let's go to the beach," but he wants to play Magic the Gathering on a Saturday because it's tournament time. So even though I don't understand the game, I drop him off, and when I pick him up, I will then take him for lunch and ask what he has done. I take an interest in the parts of what he's doing that I do comprehend, which is why I make sure to drop him. I don't send him on the bus, and I don't let him go by himself. I take that opportunity to show my interest by taking him there, and as you read in the chore game, I also use it as a tool to get him to do what he needs to do. But I do take an interest in what he's doing, and not just pay for him to go. My children know that I am interested in their lives, as opposed to controlling their lives.

Trust is a big factor as to why I do not need to control them. This trust comes from instilling truthfulness in them from an early age. I personally believe that when you lie to somebody, you actually take their power away from them. Their power to choose or make a decision on the information you've given them is what truthfulness is about. That is why I was extremely strict when it came to my children telling me the truth at all times. And it also went both ways. I told them the truth at all times. Yes, I told them in age appropriate ways, but I told them the truth because they deserve to have the power to know the information and do what they need to do with it, just like I do. So I rewarded truthfulness, and it was almost like a get-out-of-jail-free card. In my house, if something happened and I was angry about it at first, if they told me the truth about who did it and why they did it, and we had that discussion, then they actually didn't get punished. The only time they got punished was when they lied about it. I think this was again one of the biggest things that created harmony in the house, because I wouldn't get upset if they told the truth. I would sit down, discuss the consequences and what needed to be happening, and the consequence always fitted the problem that they had, so they could learn. But I could not give them a teaching moment if they didn't tell me the truth. That was a huge impact in my parenting, and I found it immensely helpful in keeping a harmonious house.

Now, some people may say that being supportive and having interest is the same as involvement, but it actually isn't. It is being involved in their lives, knowing that, and it's also not being involved in their lives. I am there when they need me and want me, and there are times when I ask them to be there when I need them. It's a give-and-take relationship, and we have to balance it out. For example, I can't always rely on my eldest child to babysit my youngest children. I mean, yes, I do need help as a single parent, but I can't ask him to forgo his life, his interests, and his goals that he needs in order to be a successful young man. I can't demand that he be involved and help me with parenting the other two kids. That's not fair for him. So, involvement changes as your rules change with your children. For example, with my youngest son, I have to be involved at this time because he's still needing that guidance, and he's still needing that teaching. He's still evolving, so my involvement is head on. With my daughter, my involvement is transitioning from being heavily involved to wanting to be involved, and sometimes needing to be involved, and there's a balance between the two. Whereas with my eldest son, who's 19, I don't need to be involved anymore. I'm involved as much as he wants me to be involved, and if I have created a positive relationship between the two of us, then that involvement is there. If they ask for it, that's when you know you've become a good parent, when your kids want you around. I appreciated my mother-in-law who did not push herself on me. She gave me the space to raise my children my way, as opposed to my mom who kept telling me, "Oh, that's not how you do it. You need to do it this way." So, we've had to work our dynamics out together, and by realizing the dynamics between my mom and me, I learned what type of dynamic I wanted with my children, and I was breaking the cycle of "too much involvement can hurt the child and your relationship," which in turn causes stress or fighting, and you don't want that— you want a harmonious home.

The last positive word is equality, and I add equity as well. Equality means giving your children everything they need to succeed, which I have discussed many times. However, let me talk more about equity. Equity is allowing your kids to participate in decision-making, and sometimes sharing that power with them. Many people who hear me speak with my kids may think that I give them way too much power. I disagree. I give them equity and hopefully they learn to do the same with their peers and in their family. I have already set my rules for my home, and we came up with some rules together, and we all know the consequences for not abiding by the rules, but true equality in the family is actioned in big decisions; for example, when it comes to moving countries. When it comes to big decisions in the family, even decorating the home or renting a new house or moving, the children should have a say. I'm not saying that you do what your children want you to do, but they should have an opinion, and they should be in on that discussion again before it happens.

The biggest part of equity when it comes to being single parents is when you're bringing a new person into the house, or you have a blended family. There are many issues when it comes to blended families, and the children's rule of equity is one of the things that you can consider to reduce the stress and fighting in a blended family, and to create harmony at home. The children will say how they feel in the appropriate way, but it's up to us to teach them how to say it, as much as what to say, and at times like that, you have to hear what they're actually saying by reading their body language. Being able to keep open communication is special, and when big changes are happening in the family, they are as affected as everybody else, and sometimes worse because, at certain ages, they don't understand the changes, and not only do they not know how to handle it, but they also might misinterpret the reason that this change is happening. So we have to be very involved in their lives, and have that equity in the home to allow them to participate, and for us to have that open door policy of communication with our children.

So, my fellow parents, you have reached the end of the book. I've given you all my gems of wisdom. So I'm going to give you some free gifts in this book, things that I do in my workshops, and I wanted to confess a personal story. In 2014, my children's and my life changed completely overnight, literally. In the morning, we had a place to live, and by that afternoon, we didn't. I tried to make it work for the sake of the children because, no matter how you feel about the other parent, or what has been done to you, or what you are going through, you have to spend more time helping your children emotionally cope with what is happening. They did not have a choice in the matter, and I didn't have a choice either, so I kind of knew how they felt, and with that, I had a lot of growing and transitioning and self-reflection to do. Fast forward six years, I went through major changes in my life, where I even moved countries for the sake of my children. I didn't need to move, but they needed to move to a better place. They were being bullied very badly, and they were unhappy. The divorce was not having a good impact on them, and they needed a clean slate.

When I made the move, I went back to school to study to be a social worker, and I had a lot of time on my hands that I never had before. Therefore, I had time to reflect on me and to analyze it. We all went through PTSD, which is a very serious thing and a very real thing. I had to receive counseling, and in turn I counselled my kids. However, there reached a certain point where I couldn't counsel them, and I needed to call in help. I wasn't embarrassed about that. As a parent, we have to know how far we can take our children and when to call for help, and they appreciate it. They've survived what they've gone through, and they've grown. I'm so proud of them, and I'm so blessed with all my heart that I was given the gifts that I've been given in order to help my children evolve. I hope what you read in this book has helped you create harmony at home, because when you create harmony at home, in a strong family, you create a strong nation.

The biggest thing that I was not doing as a parent was self-care. Ironically, while growing up, I was taught that the only way you could be a good mother was if you sacrificed everything for your children. You showed you were being a good mother when you were miserable and did not provide good self-care, and when you were completely unselfish when it came to your kids and your husband. It was the generation before me, however. I see how miserable a lot of women are in the generation before me, and how lost they are when they're supposed to die or their children leave the house and want their independence. Therefore, I chose this time in my life as a positive reflection and healing. I've learned that when really bad things happen to you, it is for a good reason, and once you're aware that the bad thing has happened, it's time to heal, and you do what is needed to heal. I'm telling you, I have an amazing village around me, and I really hope you read my acknowledgements, because you will read about each and every person in my village, what they've done in my life, and the kindness and love that I am truly grateful for. They have helped me survive in my recent years.

With this healing, I developed a game or an exercise called the affirmation alphabet. You see, I had so much negativity around me, and negative words hitting me, and if I tried to do anything good for myself, I was told I couldn't because I needed to be there for my kids, and this was from immediate family, not to mention the negative words from other people in my life. I was told that I was not allowed to have any fun because I had messed up my life with a divorce. So again, there were constant negative words, and I was believing them; because you want to believe that the people that you think love you are saying it for a good reason. Many negative words have been hidden behind constructive criticism. So I decided to do the affirmation alphabet, of which I chose a word that was positive about me, starting with every letter in the alphabet, and I said those words every morning of my life. What was really funny was that I had to also release the negativity on my birthday. I did a burning ceremony, and I wrote all those negative statements that I'd heard from all the people in the past that I felt had hurt me. But they actually didn't hurt me; they were just teaching me something. I put them on a piece of paper, and I burnt it on my birthday, and I said goodbye.

As I was going through the healing process, I looked over at my fifteen-year-old daughter. I had to go to a teacher-parent meeting, and they were telling me that she uses a lot of self-deprivation words, and that she's very negative toward herself. It hit me: Oh, my goodness, my daughter is learning from me; and here I was healing myself and changing the way I think but not including her in that process. I went home and immediately told Mckenzie that we were going to do the information about the alphabet on my birthday. We both did the burning ceremony, and then we both lit lanterns and let them go in the air. We wrote our wishes and dreams and our goals.

When she was going through a hard time, especially with people who do not understand her autism, she actually turned to me and said, "Mommy, it's okay. I used my affirmation alphabet words, and their negative words didn't matter. I told her to make sure that her positive voice is always louder than the negative outdoor voices, and she said, "Yes, I do Mommy. Thank you. So I truly hope that you can sit down with your children and do the affirmation alphabet. Each person's alphabet is different. My alphabet is different to my daughter's alphabet, so maybe take the time to personalize your alphabet and remind yourself that your positive voice should always be louder than your negative voice.

You can always go to my website, www.familycomgame.com, to get the links to my online parenting course. I do public speaking engagements, and I definitely do parent workshops and parent coaching. All the links are there. Go and get your free bonuses, and go and get your templates—and remember, I'm part of your village. You can look me up on Facebook: Interpersonal Parenting, Twitter, and Instagram @parentwithus

There, you will find templates and everything that you need to expand your learning and your family games from this book. So I'm actually going to end this book the way I end my radio show on my YouTube channel, Interpersonal Parenting, by saying, "Happy parenting!"